David Xavier Junkin

The Good Steward

Or systematic beneficence an essential element of Christianity

David Xavier Junkin

The Good Steward
Or systematic beneficence an essential element of Christianity

ISBN/EAN: 9783337260651

Printed in Europe, USA, Canada, Australia, Japan

Cover: Foto ©Lupo / pixelio.de

More available books at **www.hansebooks.com**

THE GOOD STEWARD,

OR

SYSTEMATIC BENEFICENCE

AN ESSENTIAL ELEMENT OF CHRISTIANITY.

BY

REV. D. X. JUNKIN, D.D.

"Occupy till I come."—LUKE xix. 16.

PHILADELPHIA:
PRESBYTERIAN BOARD OF PUBLICATION,
No. 821 CHESTNUT STREET.

Entered according to the Act of Congress, in the year 1864, by

THE TRUSTEES OF THE
PRESBYTERIAN BOARD OF PUBLICATION,

In the Clerk's Office of the District Court for the Eastern District of Pennsylvania.

STEREOTYPED BY WILLIAM W. HARDING.

TO THE

MINISTRY OF THE PRESBYTERIAN CHURCH;

"Stewards of the Mysteries of God,"

THIS LITTLE VOLUME,

UPON A SUBJECT VITAL IN THE CHRISTIAN SYSTEM,
INDISPENSABLE IN THE CHURCH'S WARFARE,
AND ESSENTIAL TO HER TRIUMPH,

IS RESPECTFULLY AND AFFECTIONATELY INSCRIBED BY

THE AUTHOR.

CONTENTS.

CHAPTER I.

PAGE

INTRODUCTORY. Christianity a system—A system of life—Its end the glory of God in the salvation of the Church—Every part of a system necessary—Some parts of the Christian system too much neglected—The doctrine and duty of stewardship especially—Object of this treatise stated.................. 9

CHAPTER II.

CHRISTIANITY PROVIDES, WITHIN HERSELF, THE ELEMENTS OF GROWTH AND EXTENSION. The fruit of a system usually its seed—So in religion—The provisions for disseminating religion an essential part thereof—Proof—From the nature of religion—From positive commands of Christ—From the morality of the gospel—From the marks of discipleship—From the prescribed worship of the church——The Lord's prayer... 15

CHAPTER III.

THE SCRIPTURE DOCTRINE OF STEWARDSHIP. Antiquity of the office—Definition—Explication of its duties—The doctrine and duty not peculiar to our fallen state—Announced in Eden—Foundation of the duty the sovereignty of God—This shown in the covenant of works—Unfaithfulness in stewardship the first sin... 24

CONTENTS.

CHAPTER IV.

THE DOCTRINE FARTHER UNFOLDED. Man a tenant at will—Effect of the fall upon the conditions of his stewardship—The covenant of grace an emanation of sovereignty—Holds man a steward—Alike under every dispensation—Noachic, Abrahamic, Mosaic, Christian—The doctrine both scriptural and rational—Taught in the ancient offerings—By analogy of reason.. 30

CHAPTER V

THE END AND THE MOTIVES OF STEWARDSHIP. God's glory and man's welfare the end—Reasonableness of God's claims—Harmony of this twofold end—Motives of human actions of two classes—Love and fear—One class addressed to the holy, the other to the unholy—Love the motive to beneficence—Danger of other motives... 37

CHAPTER VI.

THE RULE OF STEWARDSHIP. The word of God the rule—Every man ought to consider himself a steward of God—Ought to seek a call to his line of life—Diligence required—Perseverance in industry—" Retiring from business" unlawful—Scriptural case of such—Responsibility proportionate to "several ability"—Christ's estimate of giving—Beneficence must be cheerful—Unostentatious—Constant—Frequent—Systematic.. 43

CHAPTER VII.

SCRIPTURE PLAN OF BENEFICENCE. Stated—Proved—The plan a corollary of the doctrines—Offerings of property always a part of religious worship—This was by divine appointment—Abel offered in faith—The patriarchs—Noah—Abraham—Jacob's vow—Its principle incorporated in the Mosaic economy—Lessons of that economy—Its appropriateness and rationality—The synagogue worship—Doing alms a part of it—The dependence of the entire system of worship on the part consisting of beneficence—The spirit of worship the same under all dispensations—Mistakes refuted—What meant by a change of dispensation—The new economy aims at a vaster work, and needs ampler offerings—The compulsory feature of the ancient system removed, but the moral obligation strengthened... 50

CHAPTER VIII.

OBLATION A PART OF CHRISTIAN WORSHIP. Definition of worship—Proof of the main position from prophecy—From the fact that Christ destroyed not but completed the law—From New Testament history—Christ's example and teaching—Mary's offering and its lesson—Apostolic institutions and teaching—Judas an unfaithful steward—Primitive worship as described by Luke—Communication or fellowship—Use of the term—Christian church modeled after the synagogue—Testimony of the early fathers... 63

CHAPTER IX.

ADDITIONAL PROOFS THAT OBLATION IS A PART OF WORSHIP. From the office of deacon—Liberality of the primitive churches—The case of Ananias and Sapphira—Apostolic ordination of the system of first-day collections—The system no novelty... 77

CHAPTER X.

BENEFICENCE PART OF PRIVATE AND FAMILY RELIGION. James' definition of religion—Job's practice—Christ's example and teaching—Its happy influence in the family—And upon the church... 85

CHAPTER XI.

ADVANTAGES OF THE SCRIPTURE PLAN OF BENEFICENCE. It operates with the force of a religious obligation—Abates the force of avarice—Produces more ample results—Has the sanction of divine analogy—The power of the littles—Derives aid from other parts of Sabbath worship—Secures giving from principle and not from impulse—If God's plan, it will secure his blessing... 90

CHAPTER XII.

SYSTEMATIC OBLATION A MEANS OF GRACE AND EVANGELIZATION. God works by means—Ignorance of the *modus operandi* no objection to this—Meaning of the term grace—Oblation secures temporal prosperity—Illustrated by Israel's history—Proven by Scripture—A means of spiritual grace—Reasons for its efficacy—Object of social and fiscal inequalities—A dead level fatal—Circulation necessary to health and life—Water—Exercise necessary to growth—All the elements of piety brought into exercise in faithful stewardship—It is a means of crucifying the flesh—Especially of covetousness—The good steward characterized—Desires wealth but not for itself—Business, with him, a part of piety........................ 93

CHAPTER XIII.

OBLATION A MEANS OF GRACE AND EVANGELIZATION. Shown from the Mosaic system—One object of the ceremonial law to keep the people occupied—To restrain from idolatry—Oblation well adapted to do this—It is a means of laying up treasure in heaven—Will be mentioned at the final judgment as evidence of justification—Covetousness assigned as the ground of the curse—Necessary to the spread of the gospel............ 109

CONCLUDING APPEAL.

An Exhortation to faith and works............................. 114

unto principalities and powers in heavenly places might be known by the church the manifold wisdom of God."

To accomplish these glorious results, Christianity is a perfect instrumentality; not as a dead organism, but as a system of life, deriving its efficiency from "the Spirit of life." It is not a beautiful theory slumbering upon the sacred page, or floating unpractised in the intellect: but it is the impulse and the guide of a new life in man. Indeed we would not apply the name Christianity to the system of truth, apart from the life-giving Spirit. A human body, though perfect in its parts, is not a man, if the *soul* be absent. The system of sacred truth becomes Christianity only when, by the Divine Spirit, it is made alive and operative in the hearts and practice of believers. As our Lord is called Christ, because he is the anointed Mediator —anointed by the immeasurable unction of the Holy Ghost: so the gospel scheme becomes Christianity only by the *anointing* which abideth in the believer, and teacheth him all things. 1 John ii. 27. Christianity is "a ministration of the Spirit." 1 Cor. iii. 8. It is "the law of the Spirit of life, making free from the law of sin and death." Rom. viii. 2. The Holy Spirit is the agent, and gospel truth the instrumentality, by which "the life of God in the soul of man" is begun, developed, and perfected.

Now it is of the nature of a system, especially of a living organism, that its members are mutually dependent and jointly conduce to the designed end. In a perfect system every part is necessary. The derangement of the smallest wheel or lever may arrest the motion of a vast machine: and in a living body, "if one member suffer, all the members suffer with it." And since Christianity is a divine constitution, we must believe it to be perfect: and we ought to receive the system *entire*, and bring all its parts into normal operation. If the injunction to Moses, concerning the mere type of the system, was, "See that thou make all things according to the pattern showed thee in the mount;" and if the smallest pin or socket of the tabernacle was as necessary to the whole, as the most gorgeous of its curtains; we must not deem superfluous any of those means, by which God's ransomed ones "are builded together for an habitation of God, through the Spirit."

But has it not been the crime and the calamity of the church, that, with rare exceptions, "the law of the Spirit of life" has obtained only a partial sway? That the system, as a whole, has seldom been brought into full, free, and healthful play? Have not men too boldly dared to divide the elements of Christianity into the essential and nonessential; the important and the unimportant; assuming the prerogative of judging what parts shall have prominence, and what parts may be neglected? Has not the injunction, "prophecy according to the proportion [analogy] of faith," been too little

THE GOOD STEWARD.

CHAPTER I.

Christianity a vital system—Introductory.

The religion revealed in the Bible is a SYSTEM. Not, indeed, stated with didactic formality; but nevertheless a *system*, harmonious in its parts, and complete as a whole. To the superficial reader, its facts and doctrines may seem to lie in confusion: but it is not to the superficial observer that the systematic structure of any science is obvious. He discovers no system in the starry heavens. To him confusion seems to mark the movements of sun, and moon, and stars, and world. All seem to lie in gorgeous chaos in the bosom of night, or to move in paths confused and conflicting: whilst, to the eye of philosophy, they exhibit the perfection of order, and perform their movements with mathematical exactness. So of Christianity. To the careless glance, it may appear without form and void; whilst, to the close and prayerful student of its facts and doctrines, it presents an array of order, and beauty, and fitness.

The same Spirit who "hath garnished the heavens," hath garnished also the pages of the holy Book: and if, in the one case his work must be *studied*, in order to the disclosure of its systematic glory, so must it in the other. He, who would comprehend the perfection of order with which the planets revolve, must *study* the solar system: and he, who would discover the beauty and harmony with which each star of truth, that gems the spiritual firmament, revolves around the Sun of Righteousness, must study, with patience and prayer, the Christian system. When this is done, Christianity will be spiritually discerned, and will be seen to be "a building fitly framed together." Its facts, its doctrines, precepts, promises, and its agents and modes and means of operation, all will be discovered to be parts of a harmonious whole; mutually dependent, and jointly conducive to the glorious end to which it is adapted.

That end is the glory of God, in the salvation of his church and the aggrandizement of his eternal kingdom. And the ultimate result of this stupendous scheme will be the perfect union under Christ, and the perfect blessedness, in him, of the entire family of God—angels, principalities, powers, and ransomed men. Its grand design, as expressed by Paul to the Ephesians, is "That, in the dispensation of the fulness of times he might gather together in one all things in Christ, both which are in heaven and which are on earth; to the intent that now heeded; and have we not consequently "failed to declare *all* the counsel of God?" And has not this lack of a full and proportionate development of the elements of the new life rendered its growth sickly and distorted? We cannot doubt it, and are of opinion that, until the whole Christian system is brought into normal and complete operation, it is not reasonable to hope, that the church will " grow up into him in all things, which is the head, even Christ; from whom the whole body fitly joined together and compacted by that which every joint supplieth, according to the effectual working in the measure of every part, maketh increase of the whole body unto the edifying of itself in love." Eph. iv. 15, 16. And of all the parts of the Christian system none has been more neglected than the doctrine and the duty of *Christian stewardship*, or *evangelical beneficence.* This neglect, perhaps more than any other cause, has proved a hindrance to the success of the gospel.

Thus impressed, it shall be the aim of the writer, in the following pages, to unfold and enforce the doctrine and the duty of Christian stewardship : to show that it is an essential element of Christianity; that its principles are part of the system of Christian faith, and its duties an indispensable part of Christian practice; that it is a part of religious worship, and an important means of grace; and is therefore as strictly a portion of our holy religion as are preaching, prayer, praise, and the sacraments; that it is the element of the Christian system upon which are largely dependent the perfection of Christian character, the extension of the gospel, the triumph of the church, and the manifestation of the glory of God; and that consequently to neglect systematic beneficence is to neglect a most important part of practical piety.

CHAPTER II.

Christianity provides, within herself, the elements of her own growth and perpetuity—These are of her own essence.

WE have said that Christianity is a vital system. Now an important part of such a system is that, in which provision is made for its own growth, completion and perpetuity. An important part of vegetable organization is that which provides for reproducing and disseminating the tree or plant. For the most part it is the fruit, the useful part of the vegetable that contains its seed: and to destroy its fruit-producing organism would be to annihilate its species. And the fruit of the Spirit is the seed of the church. When, therefore, our Lord compared his kingdom to a grain of mustard seed, he taught that it contains within itself the elements of its own growth: that it embodies principles of life and extension, the development of which, like the growth of the mustard seed, will result in its own enlargement and perpetuity. And the word of God fully sustains the position that the doctrines and duties of Christian stewardship constitute that part of the religion of Christ, in which provision is made for the extension and maintainance of the whole system.

We use the term stewardship, in its most comprehensive sense, to embrace all good works, and the principles from which they spring. The faithful stewardship, the regular beneficence of Christians is at once the fruit and the seed of Christianity: it is the leaven that shall leaven the whole lump of ransomed men. It is the instrumentality by which the Holy Spirit comes on the great evangelizing work: and we say it is of the essence of the system of religion, that is taught in the Holy Scriptures. By this we mean that a man cannot be a Christian, without adopting principles and feeling motives of action, that will lead him to perform at least some of those duties, which make up the system of instrumentalities, through which Christ is to receive " the Heathen for his inheritance and the uttermost parts of the earth for his possession ;" and we further say that no society can scripturally claim to be a Christian church, that does not propose, as one object of her organization, the extension of the Christian religion. We do not say that the individual or the church, that does not do *all* that God requires, thereby forfeits Christian character. But we do say that the man, who has never felt the love of Christ constraining him to do *something* in this work, has not the proper evidence in his own heart, and affords none to others, that he is a converted man : and that the church, that does nothing in this work, ignores or rejects a part of the Christian system.

Now, Christian reader, if we shall succeed in proving these positions, from the word of God; we trust that you will promptly strive to come yourself and bring the church to which you belong efficiently up to the help of the Lord. Our statement is, that to do good to others and to labour for the world's conversion, are Christian duties; and that the performance of these duties, and the cultivation of the graces necessary thereto, are *essential parts of practical Christianity.* This we prove,

I. From the *nature of religion* as described by Christ himself. "The kingdom of heaven is like to a grain of mustard seed:" and again "the kingdom of heaven is like to leaven, which a woman took and hid in three measures of meal, till the whole was leavened." These two parables are designed to illustrate the diffusive and assimilating tendency of the gospel. True religion consists in a willing submission to the reign of heaven's King: hence it is called, in these parables, the kingdom of heaven; *i. e.* the system whereby Christ, the King of heaven, brings men to be his willing subjects, and reigns in and over them.

When that religion has been implanted in the heart, it will extend its influence, until the whole man is brought under its sway: And so in the church, so in the world. It is the *nature* of a mustard seed, when properly planted, to grow and produce the largest herb, that comes from so small a seed, so large that it offers shelter to the birds of the air. It is the *nature* of religion, when really planted in the soul, not only to grow within that soul, but to put forth its branches, to extend aid, shelter, and consolation to others. Like the mustard seed, there is in it a principle of life, which tends both to growth and propagation. It is the nature of leaven to assimilate to itself the adjacent particles of the meal, " until the whole is leavened." So it is the nature of Christianity to extend its influence in the soul, until all the powers and affections are assimilated to its own nature, and the whole man is renewed. And what is true of the individual is true of the church. It is the nature of the gospel seed, when planted in society, to grow and become a fruitful tree, offering shelter and refreshment to all around, and bearing seed for dissemination throughout the earth.

It is the nature of gospel leaven, when deposited in a community, to extend its influence and assimilate, until the whole man is leavened. If the seed, when planted, grows not, we infer that it was dead; if the leaven, when placed in moistened meal, spread not, we infer that it was not genuine. The inherent tendency of gospel religion is to universal diffusion; and the man whose religion is not of this nature, and who is not impelled, by its influence, to do something to impart it to others, ought to doubt its genuineness. We prove our position,

II. From *positive commands of Christ.* "Go ye into all the world, and preach the gospel to every creature:" taken in connection with Paul's declaration to the Romans, "How shall they hear without a preacher? And how shall they preach except they be sent?"—Christ's injunction, "Pray ye the Lord of the harvest, that he will send forth labourers into his harvest," and that of the Spirit by Solomon, "Honour the LORD with thy substance, and with the first fruits of all thine increase." These and many other similar texts are positive commands; and is it not a part of the Christian religion to obey the commands of Christ? Has that man good evidence of his piety, who lives in habitual neglect of any of his commands? Do you, reader, plead exception? So may others, and all Christians in detail, and thus Christ's work will remain undone. We maintain our position,

III. From *the nature of the gospel morality* "Therefore all things whatsoever ye would that men shall do unto you, do ye even so unto them." "Thou shalt love thy neighbour as thyself." Here is the sum of all that relates to the duty of man to man. Now, Christian, imagine yourself a pagan. Suppose you had heard, in your land of darkness, that a people, dwelling in America, possessed a book clearly attested to be a revelation from the Supreme God: a book that told of an eternal hell and an eternal heaven, and revealed the only way in which that hell could be avoided and that heaven attained, would you not desire that the Americans would send you that book and teach you the way of salvation? And if you were told that this book itself made it the duty of those who possess it to spread the knowledge it contains, would you not be amazed if no books were sent, and year after year pass, and no one came to tell you of this salvation? And would you not be still more amazed, if told that professing believers of the word of life failed to send it to you, because of their *love of money*, and eagerness for amassing worldly wealth? Have you done to others, as you would wish them to do to you if your condition were exchanged for theirs? Do you love your neighbour as yourself? Perhaps you suppose that the heathen man is not your neighbour. Go learn from the parable of the good Samaritan, that every man is your neighbour, to whom you may do good. Such is the Gospel morality: and it is part of our holy religion. The man, therefore, who neglects Christian beneficence, omits an essential part of the Christian religion. We prove our position,

IV. From *the marks of discipleship*. How are you to know that you are a Christian? "The Spirit itself beareth witness with our spirits that we are the children of God." But how is his testimony borne? By describing, in the written word, the inward graces and outward fruits which will always characterize the true believer; and by "working in us both to will and to do," thus producing the graces and the fruits by which the man is known to be a Christian. It is by this process that "our calling and election is made sure" to ourselves and others.

What, then, are those fruits, by which the Spirit witnesses that we are the children of God? We cannot detail them all here: a few will suffice. Said Paul to the Galatians, "The fruit of the Spirit is *love*, joy, peace, long-suffering, gentleness, goodness, faith." Said the beloved Disciple, "We know that we have passed from death unto life, because *we love* the brethren: but whoso hath this world's good, and seeth his brother have need, and shutteth up his bowels of compassion from him, how dwelleth the love of God in him?" "Now if any man have not the Spirit of Christ he is none of his," said Paul to the Romans; and to the Philippians he said, "Let this mind be in you that was also in Christ Jesus." And the mind or disposition here intended, is a willingness to make sacrifices for the good of others; for in the next verse he adds, "who being in the form of God * * * humbled himself and became obedient to death, even the death of the cross." And in his second letter to Corinth, the same Apostle says, "For ye know the grace of the Lord Jesus Christ, that though he was rich, yet for your sakes he became poor, that ye, through his poverty, might be rich." And Jesus himself declares, "If any man will come after me, let him deny himself and take up his cross and follow me."

Such are some of the marks of the real Christian, love, compassion, charity, goodness, self-denial for the good of others. And if you lack these, do you not lack essential parts of true religion? And we prove our statement,

V. From *the fact that part of the prescribed worship of our religion has direct reference to its own spread and perpetuity.* A separate chapter will be occupied with the proof that beneficence is a part of worship. All we shall here attempt, is to show that Christian worship contemplates the duties of stewardship and provides for the performance of them.

Prayer is a part of Christian worship and, in teaching them to pray, Christ gave to his disciples a wonderfully comprehensive summary of prayer, which embraces the substance of all that man need ask of God. The style of this prayer recognizes the social principle in worship, and intimates that "we should pray with and for others." The plural is used, "*Our* Father," not *my* father. And how much of the Lord's prayer relates to the glorifying of God, in the universal spread of the Gospel? Just one half. Three, out of the six petitions, lead us to pray that God's name may be hallowed, that his kingdom may come, and his will be done on earth as in heaven. Now if we leave out, in our regular supplications, one half of the Lord's prayer, neglecting to embrace in them one half of the topics he has commanded, do we not omit an essential part of worship? And the same is true of the omission of the prayer to the Lord of the harvest to send forth labourers into his harvest. But the man who asks God for a benefit, and yet neglects to use, according to his ability, the *means* which God has appointed for obtaining the benefit sought, "asks amiss"—does not truly pray at all.

Arguments might be accumulated. But we trust the position is sufficiently established, that the employment of the means, prescribed in the Bible, for the comfort of the poor and suffering, and for the advancement of the Redeemer's kingdom is a duty obligatory upon every Christian; and that the performance of this duty, and the cultivation of the graces necessary thereto, is an essential part of our holy religion. Of the means enjoined for this glorious purpose, the faithful stewardship of God's temporal bounty, or systematic beneficence, is an important part.

CHAPTER III.

The Scripture doctrine of stewardship.

THE office of steward is one of great antiquity. It existed in the days of Abraham, (Gen. xv. 2,) and probably at an earlier period: and in families of distinction, in the east, it exists at the present day. A steward is distinguished from an ordinary servant, in that the affairs of his master are more unreservedly entrusted to him: in the management of them, he is expected to exercise his best discretion, without minute directions from his master; he is held responsible for the prosperity of the estate, and upon that prosperity his own reward is usually made to depend; so that his interests are identified with his lord's. Under his master's general directions, the steward is a free, and therefore a responsible agent.

In the Scriptures, men are said to be stewards of God, when they are entrusted with a portion of his earthly estate, or with any of the affairs of his kingdom, to be managed for his glory and the good of his household. Thus the apostles are called

"Stewards of the mysteries of God," 1 Cor. iv. 1, being entrusted with the organization of the new economy of the church, and with the dispensation of the word and ordinances. So also a minister of religion is called "A steward of God." Tit. i. 7; Luke xii. 47. And all believers are required to be "Good stewards of the manifold grace of God," 1 Pet. iv. 10, *i. e.*, to be faithful managers of the various gifts and talents they may possess; amongst which "Manifold graces" the charitable use of property is included as is evident from the context.

In an extensive sense, then, the Christian doctrine of stewardship may be thus stated. Men have received from God, *in trust* for special purposes, all they possess; whether it be bodily or mental endowments, education, grace, social position and influence, power or property: and they are under obligations wisely, diligently, and faithfully to employ them, for the purposes specified in the deed of trust. The deed of trust is God's word; and, as we shall see, the objects specified are the glory of the Lord of all, and the good of the world. This doctrine is explicitly taught by Christ himself, in the parable of the talents, Matt. xxv. 14–30, and elsewhere; and indeed it pervades the entire Bible.

The doctrine of stewardship is not peculiar to our fallen condition. It was announced to man before the fall; and it is applicable alike to the highest and the lowest of God's intelligent creatures. The loftiest angel, as well as the lowliest man, is but a steward of his powers and possessions. Each is bound "to love the Lord his God with all his heart, and soul, and mind, and strength, and his neighbour as himself;" and a faithful stewardship, on the part of each, is but the appropriate *expression* of that love, by the performance of the duties belonging to his station and his circumstances.

The fall of man has changed the circumstances, and modified the motives of his stewardship, but it has not affected the original foundation of the duty. He is not now placed in "the garden of Eden to dress it and to keep it," but he is still in a vineyard of the Lord, planted, it is true, in a sin-blighted and barren world, but still the more loudly calling for wise and diligent culture, and yielding fruits more fragrant even, and more promotive of the master's glory, than those which clustered on the boughs of Paradise.

It may facilitate a clear conception of our subject to consider,

I. The *foundation* of the duty of Christian stewardship. It is the same with that of all moral obligation, viz., the sovereignty of God. Why am I bound to perform any duty? Because it is the will of God. But why am I obliged to obey his will? Because he is my sovereign: *i. e.*, because he is the self-existent, supreme and perfect Being, who created, upholds, and protects me; and because I am absolutely dependent upon him, and he has absolute authority over me: The basis of moral obligation, which God himself lays down, is his self-existence and sovereign authority; and under every dispensation this is presented as the *foundation* of the duty of stewardship.' In the Paradisial economy, the great lesson was: the Creator is absolute sovereign and owner; the creature is the subject and steward. Gen. ii. 8-17. It was the Lord God who planted the garden, and made the trees to grow. He "*took* the man and put him into the garden of Eden." "The Lord God commanded the man," and the command itself was an explicit assertion of sovereignty. The grant of every tree of the garden was the grant of the owner and Lord Paramount. The one tree was reserved, as a memorial of God's sovereign ownership of all: as the one day of the week had been "sanctified" as a memorial of his ownership of all man's time. The very question to be tested, in the covenant of probation, was whether man would yield implicit obedience to God as a sovereign. The thing forbidden was not in itself wrong, but indifferent. From murder or falsehood, or any thing in itself morally wrong, man's holy nature would have shrunk, and it would have been no *test*. But he could see, and it was designed he should see, no reason for obeying the prohibition except that it was the *will* of his Maker and Father: and he was put to the test, whether he would obey Jehovah's naked command, simply because he was his Sovereign.

Nor is the doctrine of stewardship less distinctly taught in this brief story of man's primal condition. He was "put" into the garden, not as absolute owner, but "to dress it and to keep it." And all the particulars, of his investiture into that beautiful estate, conclusively show that he held it as a vassal of the Lord of the whole earth; for whose glory he was bound to use it.

Nor should we fail to notice the instructive fact, that the first covenant was broken by a violation of the condition of his stewardship. God had reserved one tree, or, as some suppose, a species of tree, as an evidence of his ownership of all: and the *first sin* was a coveting of God's reserved property; a taking of God's share, in addition to that which he had freely given to man. Indeed the first sin was, in a sense, an act of unfaithful stewardship: sad type of that grasping covetousness which, in all succeeding time, has done so much to dishonour God and ruin man.

And Jehovah is not only *our* Sovereign, but also "God over all"—Sovereign of the universe—absolute owner of all things. "The earth is the LORD's and the fullness thereof: the world and they that dwell therein." Ps. xxiv. 1. "Behold the heaven and the heaven of heavens is the LORD's thy God, the earth also and all that therein is." Deut. x. 14. "The silver is mine and the gold is mine, saith the LORD of hosts." Hag. ii. 8. Man is therefore a mere tenant at will. He is absolute owner of nothing. Even he himself is not his own. He is simply a steward.

CHAPTER IV.

The doctrine of stewardship further unfolded—How affected by the fall—By the covenant of grace—The Abrahamic dispensation—The Mosaic—The Christian—Both Scriptural and rational.

WE have seen that man in innocence was a mere tenant at will of this world's goods; and if so, much more is man fallen. By the fall he forfeited life itself, and of course every other benefit; and could lay no independent claim to any possession. And although the new and better covenant, which was announced before the expulsion, makes provision for the restoration to believers of all that was lost by the fall; yet it gives no absolute and independent title to the benefits restored. The covenant of grace is itself an emanation of sovereignty; of sovereign love. It was designed, not to render man more independent of his God, nor to release him from the condition of a steward; but to bring him into a state of closer dependence, and to sweeten the duties of his stewardship, by leading him to perform them under the promptings of filial love. Accordingly under the covenant of grace, whether dispensed through the ritual law, or under the freer ministration of the Spirit, God is still the sovereign master, and man the dependent steward. In the offerings brought by the antediluvian patriarchs, they acknowledged their accountability to God as his stewards. And when, after the flood God restored to Noah the possession of the earth, and confessed a reinvestiture, the language he employs, is the language of a lord introducing his vassal to his trust-hold. See Gen. ix. 1–17.

In the Abrahamic dispensation the same great principles are prominent. The call of Abraham was the act of a sovereign; his obedience that of a faithful steward. The covenant made with him, the grant of Canaan; his payment of tithes to Melchizedek the "priest of the most high God, possessor of heaven and earth;" the sacrifice of Isaac upon God's demand, all forcefully teach the same great lesson. Gen. xii. and xxii.

And with equal distinctness and greater frequency is the doctrine of stewardship, as resting upon that of the divine supremacy, taught in the Mosaic economy. In the preface to the decalogue, God lays down the doctrine of his own self-existence and sovereignty as the basis of moral obligation. "I am JEHOVAH thy God." Exod. xx. 2. It is true he superadds, by way of special appeal to the Israelites, "Which brought thee out of the land of Egypt, out of the house of bondage:" and the fact that they "are bought with a price," adds a cord of love, ineffably tender to the bonds of duty as resting upon Christians: but the original ground of moral obligation is the sovereignty of God. Israel was bound to love and serve him, even if he had never delivered them from bondage. Man was bound to serve God even before he needed redemption: and is still so bound simply as a creature of God. In cases, almost countless, the declaration, "I am JEHOVAH"—"I am the Lord your God," is made as the foundation of obedience. See Lev. xviii. and xix. chapters. And this is adduced as the ground of obligation to obey all sorts of laws, moral, municipal, and ceremonial; and especially as the basis of the duty of charity. Lev. xix. 9, 10, and xxiii. 22.

The entire system of offerings, too, prescribed in the ceremonial law, whilst it ministered to other ends, enforced the same doctrines, and was indeed a system of beneficence. One great lesson which it taught, was that everything belonged to God, and that, therefore, we ought to "honour the LORD with our substance." The offerings for the first born, and of the first fruits, were designed to secure a systematic and perpetual acknowledgment that God is rightful owner of both the people and their property, and that all should be employed in his service and for his glory.

Nor does the introduction of the gospel dispensation render man or the tenure of his property less dependent. The gospel, as emphatically as the law, teaches the sovereignty and the claims of

Jehovah. The gentle voice of Jesus reiterates the same lesson which he had taught in Eden, and thundered at Sinai: God's sovereignty, and man's obligation. The gospel teaches that redeemed man is, if possible, more completely the property of God, and under increased obligation to serve him as a faithful steward. It assures us that the church of God, "he hath purchased with his own blood." Acts xx. 28. That "None of us liveth to himself, and no man dieth to himself; for whether we live, we live unto the Lord; and whether we die, we die unto the Lord. Whether we live therefore or die we are the Lord's: For, to this end Christ both died, and rose, and revived, that he might be Lord both of the dead and living." Rom. xiv. 7–9. It declares to believers, "Ye are not your own, ye are bought with a price, therefore glorify God in your body, and in your spirit, which are God's." 1 Cor. vi. 19, 20. If it were possible to strengthen a claim already perfect, the title of God our Saviour to his people and to all they possess would seem stronger under the gospel, than under the first covenant: for as Redeemer, and the author of "a new creation," he has added to his original claim the right of purchase.

It is true that the gospel draws men to the faithful exercise of their stewardship "with bands of love" rather than with the sterner cords of justice; yet, whilst love is the motive, the sovereign demand of God is the foundation of the duty. The law still demands the homage of men, with a voice stern as the thunders amid which it was given, and in virtue of a claim old as creation and stable as the throne of God: and whilst the gospel superadds a a more tender claim, a title sealed with blood, it relaxes not the immutable obligations of justice. To fail in the duties of Christian beneficence is, therefore, not a mere lack of gratitude. It is unfaithfulness in stewardship. It is the violation of a trust. It is the perpetration of a wrong upon our sovereign Lord.

Such is the scriptural foundation of the duty of stewardship. And, if tested by right reason, it will appear as rational as it is scriptural. Upon the universally admitted principle, that the artificer has a right to the machine, which he has invented and constructed, and to a portion at least of the products of it, our Creator has a just claim to our bodies and spirits which are "his workmanship;" and to all that we can acquire. And if we examine the history of property, and the nature of the tenures by which it is held, we will trace all valid titles up to the original grant of "the God of the whole earth," first to Adam: Gen. i. 26, and afterwards to Noah, Gen. ix.

The right to acquire property is based upon those grants; and all individual titles have grown up under that providence, of which God is the sovereign Disposer. Civil government, by which rights of property are protected, is an ordinance of God: and its various forms have arisen under his supervision. And we must not forget that, in the administration of his providential government, God is as completely sovereign, as he was in the work of creation. "He worketh all things after the counsel of his own will." Eph. i. 11. "He doeth according to his will in the army of heaven, and among the inhabitants of the earth." Dan. iv. 35. "The LORD maketh rich and maketh poor." 1 Sam. ii. 7. "He putteth down one and setteth up another," Ps. lxxv. 7.

Whence, then, reader, did you obtain your property? From your ancestors? Where did they get it? Or did you obtain it by hard labour or by skilful trade? Others have laboured as hard, and traded as skilfully as you, and are still poor. How has it come that your labour or tact in business has been more successful? You can only with truth reply, "God hath crowned my labour with success, or the efforts of my fathers; it is he has made me to differ." It is God bestows strength and skill for the struggle of life, and crowns our efforts with a blessing. In truth, by whatever means your rightful property has been obtained, it is from God. Venture not, then, to "say in thine heart, my power and the might of mine hand hath gotten me this wealth. But thou shalt remember the LORD thy God; for it is he that giveth the power to get wealth!" Deut. viii. 17, 18.

If, therefore, Jehovah is the sovereign Disposer of property, as well as its Creator and original Owner, he must surely hold man responsible for the right use of all he has committed to his care.

CHAPTER V.

The end and the motives of stewardship.

"Man's chief end is to glorify God, and to enjoy him for ever;" and the object of Christian beneficence, as of every other duty, is to subserve this chief end. Glory is the manifestation of excellence, and the grand purpose of God, in the works of creation, providence, and redemption, is to manifest his own perfections, and thus "do his pleasure," and render his creatures blessed. "The Lord hath made all things for himself," Prov. xvi. 4. "Of him, and through him, and to him, are all things: to whom be glory for ever. Amen." Rom. xi. 36. "Thou art worthy, O Lord! to receive glory and honour and power: for thou hast created all things, and for thy pleasure they are, and were created." Rev. iv. 11.

The principle here involved, that the owner has a right to promote his own honour and advantage, in the disposal and use of his property, is one which men not only admit, but eagerly assert in their own case. No man will assert that, in purchasing and maintaining horses or other domestic animals, the happiness of the animal is the chief end; but on the contrary the honour or advantage of the master. This common-sense principle men readily embrace, when it is applied to those things over which man has a partial dominion. But perhaps the very same men refuse to apply it to the more perfect dominion of God. Yet is it a dictate, alike of reason and of revelation, that the chief end of every creature is to promote the glory of the Creator. We are bound "to glorify God in our body and spirit which are God's:" 1 Cor. vi. 20; and this necessarily includes all that pertains to body and spirit; the endowments of each, and all the resources which, by their right exercise, we may procure. Of course property is included; and this might be inferred from scriptures already quoted, if there were none more explicit. But the Bible is very explicit upon this subject. "Honour the Lord with thy substance, and with the first fruits of thine increase." "Whatsoever ye do, do all to the glory of God." 1 Cor. x. 31. And space would fail us to quote a tithe of the passages, in which the right and religious use of property is required.

Upon this point bears the entire system of tithes and oblations of the ancient economy. And in 2 Cor. ix. 12, 13, the apostle, after discoursing upon the subject of Christian liberality, and specially commending the beneficence of the Macedonians, and Corinthians, declares "that the administration of this service not only supplieth the want of the saints, but is abundant also by many thanksgivings unto God, while by the experiment of this ministration, they glorify God for your professed subjection unto the gospel of Christ, and for your liberal distribution unto them and unto all men."

But in promoting the glory of God, the exercise of Christian beneficence secures also the enjoyment of him, and of the blessings of his providence and grace, both to those who give and those who receive. This will more fully appear, when we come to view faithful stewardship as a means of grace, and of spreading the gospel. It is mentioned here as one of the ends of systematic beneficence.

Having said this much of the ends, we come to speak of the *motives* which should actuate the faithful steward.

The motives by which intelligent creatures are influenced, may all be reduced to two classes. Indeed they are thus classified in the Bible, and are denominated according to their characteristics. The one class is sometimes called "*love,*" (Rom. xiii. 10; John xiv. 15; 1 Cor. xiii.,) sometimes "the Spirit of adoption." Rom. viii. 15. The other class is denominated "*fear,*" 2 Tim, i. 7, and 1 John iv. 18, and "*the Spirit of bondage to fear.*" Rom. viii. 15. This classification respects the two grand divisions into which the intellectual creation is separated, the holy and the unholy, the obedient children of God, and those who have assumed and maintain an attitude of rebellion. Into these two classes the human family is divided. The individuals of the one class have been "reconciled to God;" "born again by his Spirit," into his spiritual family; have "received the adoption of sons;" are the children of God, having "received the Spirit of adoption, whereby they cry Abba Father." That is, they look upon God with a filial feeling: they love him as children love a parent: and this feeling of love, accompanied by reverence, confidence, gratitude, and every right sentiment, prompts them to obey. "The love of Christ constraineth them." They render obedience, not from slavish dread of their Father, but from motives of love to his person and perfections and of delight in his will.

The individuals of the other class have no love to God, nor reverence for his character or his law. Their "carnal mind is enmity against God, not subject to his law:" and the only feeling, that can prompt them to render outward obedience, is fear, dread of his displeasure and its consequences. Fallen from God and into self, selfishness is their dominant impulse; not any desire to glorify God. "Devils believe and tremble." And so is it with men who have not received "the Spirit of adoption," but are still held by "the spirit of bondage to fear." They may be forced to believe "that God is and that he is a rewarder" and an avenger; but their faith doth not "work by love." They may tremble, they may fear to offend God, but they do not love to obey him.

Now we need scarcely say that love must be the motive to beneficence. That love to the divine Being and perfections, to his law, to his promises, to his people, to his cause, love for his glory, must be "the fulfilling of his law." The very word benevolence, good will, indicates that the good steward must be animated not by "the spirit of bondage to fear," but by "the Spirit of adoption." "God loveth a cheerful giver," and it is impossible that he can give cheerfully, who does not love the duty and the cause. And this is what constitutes the difference between the offerings of the mere formalist and the truly pious, the self-righteous, and the man of real charity, the Pharisee and Zaccheus, the slave and the child. The one gives from fear or pride, the other from gratitude and principle; the one from a slavish sense of disagreeable obligation, the other from the promptings of the free Spirit of adoption: the one because he fears, the other because he loves. The one kindles his zeal with dreaded purgatorial fires, the other with coals taken from the altar of burnt-offering.

The motive that is awakened by a discovery of God's wondrous mercy, "the love of God shed abroad in the heart," is the only motive that can lead to acceptable offerings. Paul assures us that this is indispensible. "Though I should bestow all my goods to feed the poor, and have not charity [love] it profiteth me nothing." 1 Cor. xiii. 3. "Faith that worketh by love" is the life of beneficence.

Our Lord cautions against motives of ostentation in alms-doing. "Take heed that ye do not your alms before men to be seen of them. Do not sound a trumpet before thee, as the hypocrites do in the synagogues and in the streets, that they may have glory of men," Matt. vi. 1, 2. Love of display is not love of Christ.

CHAPTER VI.

The rule of Stewardship.

"LORD, what wilt *thou* have me to do?" is the eager and spontaneous inquiry of every believing heart, as it submits to a sovereign Saviour. And every faithful steward of God's bounty will often ask this question, in regard to the duties of his stewardship. The word of God must furnish the answer; for it is "the only rule to direct us how we may glorify and enjoy him." Let us strive to deduce therefrom some at least of the general principles which the Lord hath prescribed for the guidance of his stewards. And,

1. Every man should endeavour to ascertain what special talent or talents have been committed to his trust; and in what department of life he is called to serve God and his generation. Every believer, indeed every individual of the human family, believer or not, ought to have a call of God to his particular vocation in life. The truth of this position is confessed by the common sense of mankind as indicated by the very structure of language. A man's business is very generally, in most languages,

denominated his "calling," his "vocation:" *i. e.*, the employment to which he is (or ought to have been) called. We do not mean that a man ought to seek, or expect an extraordinary call, like that of Abraham or of Paul. But we mean that, by due attention to the advice of parents or judicious friends, and by the prayerful consideration of his own peculiar talents and disposition, and the indications of God's word, Spirit, and providence, a man may attain a reasonable assurance, that it is his duty to pursue a given course of life. Every man in choosing his profession or calling, ought diligently and devoutly to ask, "Lord, what wouldst *thou* have me to do?" And he, who takes God's word as "a lamp unto his feet and a light unto his path," will "hear a word behind him saying, this is the way, walk ye in it." Isa. xxx. 21.

2. Diligence, in the employment, and the improvement of every talent entrusted to him, is required of every steward. The master's injunction is, "Occupy till I come." Luke xix. 13. This, literally rendered from the Greek, is, "Do business with till I come"—*i. e.*, with the talents. And the Spirit by Paul, when enjoining the very duties involved in a Christian stewardship, commands, "Be not slothful in the business." However large or small the amount of talent entrusted to him, he is bound to employ it to the best advantage. The servant who "went and hid the talent in the earth." Matt. xxv. 25, and the one who "kept the pound

laid up in a napkin," Luke xix. 20, were unfaithful stewards, they violated their trust. It was not enough that they returned what had been given, they were under obligations to improve, to " gain" for their Lord. They deserved the doom of " wicked and slothful servants." And since our Lord expressly teaches that it is the steward's duty to " do business till he come"—does it not become a serious question, whether a Christian man is at liberty to " retire from business?" Does not the very intention of retiring from business involve the purpose of hoarding up, against the day of retirement? and withholding from the current demands of charity "more than is meet?" Can a man thus accumulate wealth, who, "upon every first day of the week takes with him to the treasury, as God hath prospered him?" 1 Cor. xvi. 2, literally translated. In Luke xii. 16-21, our Lord relates, for our instruction, the story of a man who, with the design of " retiring from business," or, as the man himself expressed it, " taking his ease," had " laid up treasure for himself, and was not rich toward God." This was " a rich man," very successful in business, who had acquired so much that he was at a loss to know how to make investments; he had " no room where to bestow his goods." He was perplexed: " What shall I do?" And what was his resolution? To give to the Lord? to distribute to the poor? no, but to hoard up. " This will I do: I will pull down my barns [ἀποθήκας, *store-houses,*] and build greater, and there will I bestow [συνάξω, *gather together*] all my fruits and my goods; and I will say to my soul, Soul, thou hast much goods laid up for many years, take thine ease, eat, drink and be merry." He would retire upon his income, and take his ease—"But God said, Fool, this night thy soul shall be required of thee!" When the steward ceased to "occupy" to "do business," the Lord came! Reader, remember and ponder the moral of this parable: "So is he that layeth up treasure for himself, and is not rich toward God!"

3. Every steward will be held responsible "according to his several ability." Matt. xxv. 15. "As God hath prospered him." 1 Cor. xvi. 3. "As every man hath received the gift, so minister the same one to another, as good stewards of the manifold grace of God." 1 Pet. iv. 10. "For to whomsoever much is given, of him shall much be required," Luke xii. 48. The Master will not demand so much of him, to whom but one talent was committed, as from him who was entrusted with ten: but requires each to "do business," with the means he possesses, and faithfully to account for it. The rich steward must not measure his gifts by the offerings of the poor: nor must the poor be discouraged because he cannot equal the bounty of the rich. "If there be a willing mind, it is accepted according to that a man hath and not according to that he hath not." 2 Cor. viii. 12. In the eyes of the Master the widow, who gave two mites, exceeded in liberality

them who cast in of their abundance. In the system of Jewish offerings special provision was made for adapting the oblation to the means of the donor: and it is a fact, as instructive as it is touching, that when the mother of our glorious Lord came to redeem her first-born son, with the sacrifice demanded by the law of Moses, she offered that which the poor only might offer, "a pair of turtle-doves, or two young pigeons."

4. Beneficence must be cheerful. "Every man according as he purposeth in his heart, so let him give, not grudgingly, or of necessity: for God loveth a cheerful giver." 2 Cor. ix. 7. "Thine heart shall not be grieved when thou givest, because that for this thing the Lord thy God shall bless thee in all thy works, and in all that thou puttest thy hand unto." Deut. xv. 10. "If there be a willing mind it is accepted." 2 Cor. viii. 12.

The necessity for this rule we have shown, when speaking upon the motives of beneficence; and the Scripture quoted is so explicit that it needs no farther illustration.

5. Christian beneficence should be unostentatious. We have already touched upon this rule, also, in speaking of the motives that should actuate the good steward. "Do not sound a trumpet before thee," —a proverbial expression for "Do not make a display." "When thou doest alms, let not thy left hand know what thy right hand doeth." Matt. vi. 3. This also is a proverbial mode of describing

such secrecy as to escape, if possible, the observation of our own hearts; and it is designed to guard against pride-fostering self-gratulation. The import of the entire precept is, that we should, when doing good, be so absorbed with the desire to honour God, that self will be forgotten.

We do not suppose that it is a positive injunction to conceal our beneficence in all cases; for that were impossible: and this would conflict with directions given in the previous parts of our Lord's sermon. "Let your light so shine before men, that they may see your good works, and glorify your Father which is in heaven." Matt. v. 16. Absolute secrecy is not always practicable nor desirable. Yet if our good works are seen, it should be manifest that they were not done merely to be seen; for ostentatious benevolence will bring no glory to our Father. And there is perhaps no more insidious or dangerous temptation, than that of being proud of our beneficence, or of making a righteousness of it. And the best antidote to this temptation is an absorbing zeal for God's glory. If beneficence is not practised with a self-denying spirit, and in a pride-crucifying manner, instead of proving a means of grace, it will prove a most specious and ruinous snare. It is worthy, therefore, of very serious consideration, how far the plans of benevolent operation, that have been in vogue in our day, have fostered an ostentatious spirit in the church, by the parade of names, the pomp of anniversaries and other seeming violations of our Lord's directions: how far the spirituality of the church may have suffered in consequence; and how far God's blessing upon her efforts may have been forfeited.

6. Christian beneficence should be constant, frequent, and systematic. But as this will of necessity be involved in the discussion of other parts of the subject, we detain not our readers with it at present. Indeed we have already shown, that beneficence, in common with the other provisions made in the gospel, for doing good to men and evangelizing the world, is an essential part of our holy religion. If so, we have no more right to intermit the performance of this, than of any other religious duty, and in the performance of it should be *systematic*, for, in religion, " all things should be done decently and in order." 1 Cor. xiv. 40.

CHAPTER VII.

The Scripture plan of beneficence.

In examining this part of the subject, let us not forget that "all Scripture is given by inspiration of God, and is profitable, for doctrine, for reproof, for correction, for instruction in righteousness: that the man of God may be perfect, thoroughly furnished unto all good works," 2 Tim. iii. 16, 17, and the Scriptures embraced in this remark more especially, were the Scriptures of the Old Testament: for these only could Timothy "have known from a child;" the New Testament not having been then written. So that, when seeking to be "thoroughly furnished unto all good works, we must consult the whole Bible, the Old as well as the New Testament. Now we think it is perfectly demonstrable that the Bible makes the belief of the doctrines, the cultivation of the graces, and the practice of the duties of Christian stewardship to be of the essence of the true religion: and requires the frequent, stated, and systematic contribution of a portion of worldly substance to pious uses, as a part of the worship of God. This is the Bible system of beneficence. Let us to the proof.

If the doctrines of stewardship, as stated in the preceding pages of this treatise, be true, and we think ample proofs of their truth have been given, then the above proposition follows as a necessary inference. The plan is a corollary of the doctrines. But in further proof and illustration notice,

1. Under the Old Testament dispensation, both in the patriarchal and the Mosaic economy, frequent, stated, and systematic oblation of worldly substance is recognized as a part of religious worship. In the first family, offerings of property were made to the Lord; Gen. iv. 3; and we are assured, upon New Testament authority, that they were of divine appointment. It was "by faith Abel made a more acceptable sacrifice than Cain." He believed. What did he believe? God's command and promise, authorizing the offering. This is the only way in which he could be said to offer in faith. And there must have been some divine directions given to the patriarchs concerning these forms of worship; else they would have been unauthorized acts of will-worship, not made in faith. But their worship was "by faith," and the offerings of the patriarchal worshippers were therefore the requirements of a revealed religion. They are said by Paul "through faith and patience to inherit the promises," and we are exhorted by him to be "followers of them." Heb. vi. 12. Even when the church was tossed in the ark, upon a shoreless ocean, arrangements were made for the family of

Noah, by divine direction, for "honouring the Lord with their substance." Of clean beasts, such as were suitable for sacrifice, Noah was directed to take by sevens, and of unclean only by two. And the first act of the patriarch, after leaving the ark, was to build an altar and take of every clean beast and of every clean fowl, and offer burnt-offerings upon the altar. Gen. vii. 20, and viii. 20.

Abraham gave tithes of all to "the priest of the most high God, possessor of heaven and earth." Gen. xiv. 20. Jacob's vow, recorded Gen. xxviii. 22, was doubtless made in faith, for it was made just after Jehovah had revealed himself to him in a dream, and renewed to him the promise given to his grandfather; and this vow embodies the whole doctrine of stewardship as we have stated it. "Of all that thou shalt give me, I will surely give the tenth unto thee!" He confesses that all the property he might acquire would be God's gift; and he solemnly vowed that he would systematically devote a tenth to the Lord. And we are of the opinion, that this vow was made by Jacob, as a public person, and that it bound his household, the future church; for it was made in response to the reiteration of the *charter* of the ancient church. This charter had been announced to his grandfather, repeated to his father, and reiterated and confirmed to himself, in the sweetly-awful scene from which he had just arisen: "In thee and in thy seed shall the families of the earth be blessed." Gen. xii. 3;

xxii. 18; xxvi. 4. It was in response to this that Jacob's vow was made, and therefore we think it included at least the religious society that was to spring from "his loins." And this opinion is strengthened by the fact that when his descendants were fully organized under this general charter, as the visible church, the principles of the vow were incorporated into the Mosaic economy. "And all the tithe of the land, whether of the seed of the land, or of the fruit of the tree, is the Lord's: it is holy unto the Lord. And, concerning the tithe of the herd, or of the flock, the tenth shall be holy unto the Lord." Lev. xxvii. 30–32. This was in addition to the first fruits and their attendant offerings, for it was after these were deducted, that the tenth was to be given to religious purposes. And if the reader will study the Mosaic system of offerings, the burnt-offerings, the meat-offerings, the drink-offerings, the peace-offerings, the contributions attendant upon the three great annual feasts, the free-will offerings, and the regular sacrifices and such as were required upon special occasions, he will discover, that offerings of property, as an expression of faith in God and his promises, trust in Messiah and his grace, gratitude for temporal benefits and saving mercy, dependence upon God as an exhaustless portion, and submission to God as a sovereign King, made up a large, if not a chief part of their public worship. And he will discover, too, much more rationality in their ceremonial system, than some are willing to attribute to it. It was an appropriate expression before the Lord, of the worshipful sentiments, which they cherished, and it was a well-appointed means of cherishing those sentiments.

What is worship? It is the cherishing in the heart true faith in God, and proper sentiments of love and veneration for him; and giving appropriate expression of these sentiments by outward acts or forms. Beings constituted as we are cannot worship God socially without some outward forms. Thought and feeling cannot be communicated from mind to mind without some material medium. Language itself is a material medium of thought, and if nothing but words were employed to express religious sentiment, it would still be a form of expression. The emotions and thoughts of the heart must be bodied forth, before they can fix the attention and engage the sympathies of others. Hence, from a necessity arising out of the constitution of our nature, a religion adapted to man, to be used in social worship, must be, like himself, composed of soul and body; of sentiments of the mind, and suitable forms by which these sentiments may be expressed. Even in private worship, the form is not useless, the attitude of the body, the tone of the voice, the action of the outward man, may assist, not only in expressing the pious emotions of the heart, but in awakening proper emotions and giving them intensity. This we believe to be the experience of every Christian.

Now what more explicit and approprite expression of faith, confidence, love, gratitude, zeal, humility, dependence, submission, and obedience, than the offering to God, in honour of him, for the support of his servants, for the maintenance of his religion, and for the comfort of his poor, oblations of that worldly substance, of which he is the maker, the giver, the owner? No outward act could more emphatically express these religious sentiments, than the act of *offering*, for, when performed aright, all these sentiments must combine to produce the act. We speak not now of sacrifices strictly so called, such as were designed to make atonement for ceremonial sins, and thus to point to the sacrifice of Christ. These eloquently expressed the religious sentiments of faith in Messiah, love to him, penitence for sin, and abhorrence of it: but as these were sacrificed, *i. e.*, destroyed by burning or otherwise to express the destroying nature of sin, they do not so strictly come under the denomination of beneficence. Still they were offerings of property, and to some extent teach the same great lesson, viz., that the worship of the ancient church, with a beautiful propriety, consisted largely in offerings of property for sacred and charitable purposes: that it was indeed a system of beneficence.

All their acts of public worship were to be accompanied by a contribution. The command is often reiterated, "They shall not appear before the Lord empty." Deut. xvi. 16; Ex. xxiii. 15, and

xxxiv. 20. The first-fruits, the tenths, the gleanings, and the sin-offering were obligatory: others were free-will offerings. Yet whilst in these neither the amount nor the frequency was always prescribed, the command was positive. "Thou shalt not harden thy heart, nor shut thine hand from thy poor brother; but thou shalt open thine hand wide unto him." Deut. xv. 7, 8.

And we know from unquestionable authority, that after the general adoption of the synagogue worship, the general principles of their benevolent system were incorporated in the forms of that worship. In this place of worship they did not feel at liberty, any more than at the temple, to " appear before the Lord empty." And the "doing of alms," as well as reading the law, preaching or expounding, praise, and prayer, was a regular part of the synagogue worship. For attending to collection and distribution they had their *Tsedpheh gebai*, διαχόνοι, *deacons*, as well as their other officers to teach and to preside over the worship; collections were usually made every Sabbath, and besides these they had sometimes extraordinary collections. Two chests for the reception of money were kept, usually, in every synagogue. Therein the money was deposited, and when extraordinary collections were to be made, "then," says Leo of Modena, "the heads of the synagogue order the *Chazan* to go to each member of the congregation, and to get their names for alms in this form, 'May the Lord bless N., who will spend so much in alms for this or that purpose.'" In the time of our Lord's advent the custom of "doing alms in the synagogues," Matt. vi. 3, was continued, as indeed it is to this day; and it was and is done as a part of the worship, as we shall presently see.

It is manifest, therefore, from an inspection of the entire Old Testament economy, and from authentic accounts of the practice of the church of Israel, that pious beneficence was statedly, frequently, and systematically practised, as a part of moral duty and religious worship. And we desire it to be distinctly remembered, that the offices of beneficence were so completely part of their worship, as to be inseparable from it. Their offerings were not matters which might be omitted, and the worship of God be still carried on. Stop these, and the entire system of their public solemnities ceased.

"But," it will be said, "Hebrew worship is not Christian worship." It is not in form: but it is so in fact. It is not so in shadow, but it is in substance. The church under the ancient dispensation was the same blood-bought church; she was gathered under the same charter, she worshipped the same God, she trusted in the same Messiah, and the same grand results were contemplated, as under the new: and although some of the forms of worship have, for obvious reasons, been changed, the spirit and the purposes of worship are unchangeably the same. We too easily release ourselves from the obligations of Old Testament precepts, by the erroneous assumption, that as the old dispensation has passed away, we have little or nothing to do with its teachings. What does Christ himself declare upon this subject? "Think not that I am come to destroy the law and the prophets: I came not to destroy but to fulfil." Matt. v. 17. The system of ceremonies, which was chiefly designed to keep in remembrance the promise of Messiah's advent, and to figure forth the doctrines of salvation through him, has ceased. The sacrifices, strictly so called, have been superceded by his coming; but these only. They have given place to the simpler ceremonies, that remind us of the fact that he has come and suffered. But all the parts of the ancient economy, that are of moral obligation, are as binding upon the human conscience as ever. And all the ceremonial and municipal laws of the Israelites, that were of permanent advantage to human society, and that are calculated to subserve the interests of God's glory in all time and in all lands, are still binding in their spirit, if not in their form. For example, such ceremonial or municipal laws, as were designed to promote public cleanliness and health, in a city or a camp, though not binding in their precise form or strict letter, are yet binding in their spirit, and Christians ought to make conscience of reducing their principles to practice. The form and the penalty of a divine law may be changed, but its moral spirit never dies. Before we can feel at liberty to cast aside any Old Testament institution, we must be convinced that it was designed to accomplish some specific temporary end, and that such end has been accomplished; that it was confined to the Jewish state, and to Judea, and is inapplicable to other nations, countries, and times; that it pertained to that yoke of bondage which was peculiar to the non-age of the church, and which Christ has removed; or that it was strictly sacrificial and pointed to a Saviour yet to come, and has therefore been superseded by his advent. Indeed the safe rule is to receive as still binding in spirit every law, unless there can be shown an explicit or an implied repeal. We say in its spirit, for there may be a repeal of the form, whilst the spirit remains. The prescribed forms of offering property under the old economy were designed to subserve temporary ends, and as those ends have been accomplised, the peculiar ceremonies attending the offering have been abolished. But has the duty of offering been abolished also? By no means. We might as well insist that public prayer is abolished, because the altar of incense has been removed; that the Sabbath has been abolished because the day has been changed, or that the law against adultery has been abolished, because the penalty has been mitigated.

The spirit of true religion is immutable, for it is the Spirit of the Lord dwelling in the heart of man:

and the ancient law of offerings "was a schoolmaster to lead us to Christ," not only that we might be justified by faith, but that by faith we might live to the Redeemer's glory, offering "our bodies a living sacrifice, holy and acceptable unto God."

What do we mean, when we speak of a change of dispensation? The word dispensation in every place in which it occurs in the New Testament, is in the Greek, *economy*, οικονόμια, *stewardship;* e. g. Eph. i. 10, "the dispensation of the fulness of times;" iii. 2, "dispensation of the grace of God." All we can mean, then, when we speak of a change of dispensation, is a change of economy, of stewardship, a change of the external form under which true religion is administered, a change of the mode in which God's grace is dispensed, and, to some extent, a change as regards the stewards employed, and the persons to whom the grace is offered. Before the ascension of Christ, the stewardship was confined to a single nation, and the offers of salvation chiefly confined to them. But now the stewardship has been changed both as regards its objects, its agents, and the mode of its administration. The wall of separation is broken down, Jew and Gentile are alike welcome to share in the stewardship and its benefits; and the guidance of God's "free Spirit" has superseded the teachings of the legal "schoolmaster." But although the form of the stewardship has been thus changed, and an ampler and freer economy introduced, it is still "the dispensation of the grace of God," and its object now, as of old, is to bring men "to the blood of sprinkling."

If the New Testament economy aims to accomplish a vaster work than did the old; if its "field is the world," its means ought to be proportionate to the vastness of the enterprize; and we might expect that, in the system itself, provision would be made for augmenting the means. We cannot suppose that, under a dispensation so much more free and full, a dispensation of love, the provisions for sweet charity would be less perfect than under the old. It cannot be that, where so much more is given, less will be required. Although, therefore, the compulsory feature of the ancient system of beneficence is removed, and men may no longer (as we believe) be required by law, either civil or ecclesiastical, to "bring tithes into the storehouse" of the Lord; yet are we fully convinced, that the obligation to be systematically beneficent is rather strengthened than relaxed; and that the motives thereto are increased in tenderness and power. If Christ has removed the yoke of ceremonial observances, he has not destroyed, but completed those parts of the law and the prophets, which, being of permanent and universal utility, are perpetually binding. If Jesus has called his people unto liberty, it is not that they may "use liberty for an occasion to the flesh, but may by love serve one another."

Gal. v. 13. Accordingly we find the New Testament not only abounding with the doctrine and duties of Christian stewardship; but it not obscurely teaches that it is a part of religious worship that should be as statedly and systematically observed as any other.

CHAPTER VIII.

Systematic beneficence a part of Christian worship.

LET the reader keep in mind the definition of worship already given, viz., the cherishing in the heart faith in God, and proper sentiments of love and veneration for him; and the appropriate expression of these sentiments by outward acts or forms. This, when performed according to God's revealed will, is true worship; and we maintain that the gospel plan of benevolence is to secure the frequent and systematic "doing of alms," by retaining it as a part of the regular worship of God. It is a part of the Christian worship, as it was of the Israelitish, to express their faith, love, gratitude, zeal, humility, submission, and other pious sentiments, by bringing offerings to the Lord. We propose to prove, first, that it is a part of regular public worship, and then, that it is also a part of family and private religion. And our difficulty is, not to find a sufficient number of Scriptures to prove our position, but to make a proper selection, so as not unduly to cumber our pages and weary the reader. We prove it,

I. From the fact that the Old Testament prophecies

contemplate the bringing of gifts and offerings to the Lord, as a part of the worship of God, in the times of Messiah. Isaiah, chap. lx., in predicting gospel times, and the calling of the Gentiles, declares " They shall bring gold and incense, and they shall show forth the praises of Jehovah. * * * All the flocks of Kedar shall be gathered together to thee, the rams of Nebaioth shall minister unto thee. * * * Surely the isles shall wait for me, the ships of Tarshish first, to bring thy sons from far, their silver and their gold with them, unto the name of the Lord thy God." Indeed the whole chapter is descriptive of the abundance of the means, that shall be furnished by Christian liberality, for the support of the church and the advancement of God's glory. And let it be particularly observed, that these offerings were to be made in connexion with prayer, " incense," and are represented to be " unto the name of the Lord God ;" *i. e.*, is as a worshipful expression of their veneration for his name. Zechariah, predicting the coming of Christ, and the day when " the Lord shall be King over the whole earth," speaks of the " gathering together of the wealth of the Heathen, and gold and silver and apparel in great abundance." Zech. xiv. 14. By Malachi also, i. 11, the Lord declares, " From the rising of the sun unto the going down of the same, my name shall be great among the Gentiles: and in every place incense shall be offered unto my name and a pure offering." " My name shall be great" means

"I shall be worshipped"—and he specifies by adding that "incense"—*i. e.*, praise and prayer, "shall be offered" in every place, and a pure offering. For, comparing this passage with Ps. cxli. 2, and Rev. v. 8, and viii. 3, we learn that incense denotes praise and prayer. Thus have we a prediction that under the gospel, prayer, praise, and pure offerings shall be made. And as we know that no strictly sacrificial offerings are lawful, these can only be offerings of "the first-fruits of our increase" to the honour of God, and they are to be offered as part of religious worship. Accordingly, the duties of Christian beneficence are, in the New Testament, expressly called sacrifices. Heb. xiii. 16. "But to do good and to communicate (contribute) forget not for with such sacrifices God is well pleased." And Paul quotes the ceremonial law, as authority for the duty of contributing to the support of the ministry. 1 Cor. ix. 9, 10, 13, 14. "It is written in the law of Moses, thou shalt not muzzle the mouth of the ox that treadeth out the corn. Doth God take care of oxen? Or saith he it altogether for our sakes? For our sakes, no doubt, this is written. Do ye not know that they which minister about holy things, live of the things of the temple, and they which wait at the altar are partakers of the altar? Even so hath the Lord ordained, that they which preach the gospel should live of the gospel."

II. Christ "hath not destroyed, but fulfilled" that part of the law and the prophets, which contemplated the continuance of devout offering of property to the Lord, as a part of religion. This part of worship is not abrogated in the New Testament, but is repeatedly enjoined as a religious duty : for,

(*a.*) The very first act of worship, that is recorded in the New Testament, as offered to the infant Jesus, was accompanied by oblations of property. The wise men " fell down and worshipped him ; and, when they had opened their treasures, they presented (margin, *offered*) unto him gifts, gold, frankincense and myrrh." And these men, we are told, were " warned of God" in their proceedings. This is a literal fulfilment of prohecy. See Ps. lxxii. 10, 15. and Isai. lx. 6.

(*b.*) Christ himself, whilst a member of the Jewish Church, and " in the condition of a servant," (Phil. ii. 7,) set us the example of offering ; for, in this respect, he " fulfilled all righteousness."

(*c.*) In the sermon upon the mount, the object of which is to present an abridgement of the principles of his kingdom, and to correct the erroneous glosses that had been put upon the law of God, Christ, so far from abrogating the law of faithful stewardship, reasserts it, and expounds the true principle of alms-giving. In Matt. vi. 1–18, he mentions " alms-doing" as a part of religious worship : " Take heed that ye do not your piety* [or religion-righteousness] before men, to be seen of

---

* Griesbach and the best critics retain δικαιοσυνην as the true reading.

them," v. 1. This is a general precept not to be ostentatious in acts of worship: and in the following verses several parts of worship are specified, and directions are given concerning the spirit and manner in which they should be performed. Almsdoing, prayer, fasting, and so on, are mentioned in their order. Now these directions were given to his disciples; (for it was they he was teaching—see chap. v. 1, 2;) and it is proof positive, that he expected them to practise these parts of religion. In this sermon also, we have proof, that alms-doing was a part of the synagogue service; and a very strong presumption is here created, that Christ designed that his disciples should model the Christian worship after that service. For he does not suggest any change in the form, but only the spirit and manner with which the hypocrites observed it.

(d.) Christ sanctioned the pious offering of property in his service, permitting many of his female followers, and others, to "minister unto him of their substance," although he might have supplied his own and his disciples' wants, by miracle. Indeed from the very first, there seems to have been a common treasury in the family of our Lord; for we are told that Judas "had the bag [literally the casket, or box] and bare what was put therein;"* and that, under Christ's directions, he was in the habit of purchasing necessaries. Indeed, Judas

* Literally "things cast in," or contributions. John xii. 6, and xiii. 29.

seems to have been the steward, or treasurer of the household : and if he was unfaithful, and appropriated to himself a part of his Lord's funds, his dreadful doom should prove a warning to all others, to avoid the sin of unjust stewardship.

(*e.*) Christ taught his disciples when he sent them forth to preach, to rely upon the offerings of the people for their support: "for the workman is worthy of his hire." Luke x. 7.

(*f.*) Christ emphatically commended the costly offering of spikenard ointment which the pious Mary brought, to anoint his feet. She had kept it, as he tells us, "against the day of his burial," though, most likely, the gentle worshipper knew not the full meaning of what she was doing. She was sweetly inclined " to work a good work upon him," she scarce knew how or wherefore, it may be. But Jesus, whose Spirit inclined her thereto, commended her : " She hath done what she *could*, she is come beforehand to anoint my body to the burying." Mark xiv. and John xii. The covetous Judas was indignant, and could see no propriety in "this waste." He had a sudden fit of charity for the poor, as many have, who can see no use in anointing Christ's body, and who make a pretended love for the poor the excuse for withholding contributions for evangelical purposes. But the Lord judged differently ; and predicted that the story of Mary's beneficence should accompany the announcement of the gospel in all lands, and in all time. And is there no object in this, besides being "a memorial of her?" Is the universal spread and perpetuity of this story designed to accomplish no higher object than to impart to an humble female a deathless fame? Surely it has. It is designed to teach all men, "wherever this gospel is preached, throughout the world," that it is "a good work" to contribute to anoint the body of Christ; to worship him in the devout bestowment of those means whereby "the anointing which teacheth all things and is truth," 1 John ii. 27, may be imparted to the whole chosen race; to offer those oblations of prayer, property, and labour, which are demanded for the great evangelizing work; so that "his body, which is the church," Eph. i. 23, may be anointed with the Holy Ghost; and so that its members, like its glorious Head, may be buried in trust, and raised in triumph! But, in the narrative of this touching scene at Bethany, we are also taught, that the church "shall have the poor always with her, and whenever she will, she may do them good." Mark xiv. 7. She will never be deprived of objects of charity, nor of the luxury of doing good. This means of grace will never be taken from her, whilst she is in her militant state. But we prove our position,

III. From the fact that the Apostles, to whom "the dispensation of the Gospel was committed" at first, and who, under the inspiration and guidance of the Holy Ghost, organized the New Testament church, and gave form to its worship, taught the doctrines and duties of Christian stewardship, and retained systematic beneficence as a part of the worship of God.

Of the many proofs of this we can offer but a few. We have already seen that Christ intimated in the sermon on the mount, that it would be so. And that they carried out his directions, we have proof,

1. In Acts ii. 42, where the worship of the primitive congregations is described. "And they continued steadfastly in the apostles' doctrine, and fellowship, and in breaking of bread, and in prayers." In this verse, communicating of worldly substance is mentioned as part of religious worship. But as this is not at first obvious to the English reader, some exegetical explanation is needed. Notice then,

As Christ, at his baptism, had been pointed out, by the descent upon him of the Spirit of God, as the Head of the church beloved of the Father: see Matt. iii. 18, 17, compared with Isai xlii. 1; so, on the day of Pentecost, by the baptism of the Holy Ghost, the disciples were designated and endowed as the visible church, the body of Christ. This awfully interesting scene the historian describes in the first part of this chapter. He then reports the substance of Peter's sermon, and the effect it produced under the power of God's Spirit: thousands convinced of sin and inquiring, "Men and brethren, what shall we do?" He then states that three thousand were the same day added to the church; which, with the five hundred brethren previously associated, constituted the primitive Christian church at Jerusalem. And it is of this church the historian says, in the fourteenth verse, that they continued steadfastly in the apostle's doctrine, and in fellowship, and in breaking of bread, and in prayers."

This is a brief description of their mode of worship; which consisted of four distinct parts, viz., the doctrine of the apostles, *i. e.*, preaching and instruction; fellowship or communication; the breaking of bread, *i. e.*, the Lord's supper; and prayers. Now the second of these we believe to be the communication or contribution of money or other property for the general expenses of religion and the support of the poor. The Greek word translated fellowship, is *koinonia*, κοινωνία, and it means communication, participation, fellowship in any benefit. The verbal form of the word means to communicate, to impart, to participate. In this place it cannot denote partaking of the Lord's Supper, for that is designated by the separate phraseology, "the breaking of bread." Neither can it mean fellowship with the apostles, in the way of social intercourse, for that is an unauthorized sense of the word; and the apostles could not be socially intimate with such a multitude. And the construction of the entire sentence presents, to the eye of the Greek scholar, such a separation of the phrase "fellowship," from the preceding and succeeding words, as to give it a distinct and independent meaning. The conjunction and the article are both repeated, which is not done when words are in apposition, καὶ τῇ κοινωνίᾳ. To get the true force of the construction, it must be read, "the doctrine of the apostles, and the fellowship or communication, and the breaking of bread, and the prayers." We think, therefore, that the historian designed to inform us that communication, or pious beneficence, was observed in the primitive congregations, as part of their worship; just as it had been in the synagogue service, to which these converts had been accustomed.

The use of this word [κοινωνία] in other parts of the New Testament authorizes the above interpretation. Look at a few examples. "For it hath pleased them of Macedonia and Achaia to make a certain *contribution* [κοινωνία] for the poor saints which are at Jerusalem." Rom. xv. 26. In his second epistle to the Corinthians, ix. 13, Paul, in urging believers to liberality, says, "They glorify God, for your professed subjection to the gospel of Christ, and for your liberal *distribution* [κοινωνίας] unto them and unto all men." In Phil. iv. 15, the apostle uses the verbal form of the word, when speaking of his departure from Macedonia, in the same sense, "no church communicated with me [ἐκοινώνησεν] concerning giving and receiving but ye only." "Take upon us the fellowship [κοινωνίαν] of ministering to the saints." 2 Cor. viii. 4. In the charge, in which Timothy is enjoined to give to "the rich in this world, that they be rich in good works, ready to distribute, willing to *communicate*," 1 Tim. vi. 17, 18, the word is used in the same sense. In Heb. xiii. 16, the same word is used in such a connection, as to show that its gospel sense is fellowship in one another's resources, *i. e.*, distribution, beneficence; and also that κοινωνία is a part of religious worship. Let the reader turn to the passage, and he will see, that in verse 12, the apostle had spoken of the sacrifice of Christ, who, "that he might sanctify the people, with his own blood, suffered without the gate." "By him, therefore," urges he in the fifteenth verse, "let us offer the sacrifice of praise to God continually, that is, the fruit of our lips, giving thanks to his name." "But," adds he in verse sixteen, "to do good and to communicate, forget not, for with such sacrifices God is well pleased." Here notice, (*a*.) "to do good" and "to communicate" are nouns, in the Greek *eupoiias and koinonias,* εὐποιίας καὶ κοινωνίας ; so that literally rendered, it is "But forget not welldoing, and communication, (*koinonias.*) (*b*.) Beneficence and communication, or contribution, are called New Testament sacrifices, and are mentioned in connection with praise and thanksgiving as parts of worship. The above array of passages, in which this word is used, proves that its New Testament sense is communication, or contribution, and that Luke designs to say, in Acts ii. 42, that one part of the worship of the primitive Christian congregations was "contribution," and that therefore their beneficence was frequent and systematic. This view is confirmed too by the classic use of the word. Schleusner, and other lexicographers of the first authority, give the senses "communication of benefits, liberality, beneficence, alms, collection for the poor." Calvin also in commenting on the place, remarks, "Luke doth not in vain reckon up these four things, viz., attending upon the word, contribution, the Lord's Supper, and prayers, when he describes to us the well-ordered state of the church." These views will be strengthened when we consider our next proof.

2. The Christian church and its worship was modelled after the synagogue service of the Jews. We have shown in a preceding section, that the synagogue worship consisted in part of contributions, and that they had officers, *diakonoi*, to receive and distribute the gifts of the worshippers. To this form of worship all the original members of the primitive church had been accustomed; and we have both scriptural and historical evidence, that the same system of worship, with such modifications only as their new circumstances demanded, was transferred to the Christian congregations.

That the practice of bringing offerings, in connexion with their acts of worship, obtained in the primitive church, is proven both by the testimony of the early fathers and by Scripture.

Justin Martyr, who wrote his Apology for the Christians about A. D. 140, after explaining their views of the sacraments, says, " On the day which is called Sunday, there is an assembly in one place, of all who dwell either in towns or in the country, and the writings of the apostles or of the prophets are read, as long as time permits. Then when the reader has ceased, the president or pastor delivers a discourse, in which he instructs the people, and exhorts to carry into practice such lovely precepts. At the conclusion of the discourse, we all rise up together and pray. Then, when the prayer is ended, as we have already said, bread is brought, and wine and water,* and the president, as before, offers up prayers and thanksgiving with all the fervency he is able; and the people express their assent by saying, Amen. The consecrated elements are then distributed and received by every one, and a portion is sent by the deacons to those who are absent. Each of those who have abundance and are willing—for every one is at liberty—contributes what he thinks fit, and what is collected is deposited with the president, who succours the fatherless and the widows; and those who are in necessity, from disease or any other cause; such as are in bonds, and strangers that come from afar —and in a word he is the guardian and almoner

---

* Probably to dilute the wine, which was sometimes kept in a thick state, and before being drunk was " mingled." See Prov. ix. 2, " Wisdom—hath mingled her wine."

to all the indigent." Tertullian, who addressed an Apology for the Christians to the Governess of Proconsular Africa about A. D. 200, bears a similar testimony: but we deem it unnecessary to occupy space with quotations. [See Reeves' Apologies.]

The testimony of these writers, one of whom lived almost contemporary with the last of the apostles, goes to prove that the early churches had adopted the mode of worship of the synogogue, and that contribution was a part thereof. It throws light also upon the Scripture declaration relating to this subject, and accords with the general tenor of Scripture usage.

CHAPTER IX.

Additional proofs that oblation is a part of Christian worship.

The last chapter was occupied with proofs of the position that beneficence is a part of Christian worship; and as we deem this position of great importance we will add some other evidence.

3. Our third argument is based upon the fact that, at an early period, the office of deacon or minister of alms, which had existed in the synagogue, was established by the apostles, in the primitive church. Finding that attention to this, in connexion with the other parts of the church service, rendered their labours too burdensome, they established this order of officers, for the very purpose of securing and distributing the offerings of the people. These officers were elected by the people, and solemnly ordained with the laying on of hands to "this business." The office was introduced into all the churches, and was evidently designed to be perpetual; for Paul, in his first letter to Timothy (iii. 8–13), describes the qualifications of deacons, and the advantage that is to be derived from the right exercise of the office. Now we

argue that, if officers are to be ordained in the churches "over this business," the business itself is a part of the service of the church. And this argument is strengthened by a consideration of the reasons which the apostles assigned for the institution of the office, viz., " but we will give ourselves continually to prayer and the ministry (deaconry) of the word." The Apostles and other " pastors and teachers" attended to the "prayers and the ministry of the word," the *diakonoi* to the ministry of collection and distribution. All were ecclesiastical officers, all officiated in the worship of the church, the one class as ministers of prayer and the word, the other class to the ministry of alms.

4. Liberality is frequently mentioned as a prominent characteristic of the primitive Christians. So constant and faithful were they in this part of worship, that they are represented as having all things common. Acts ii. 44, 45, and iv. 32, 37. This is commended as part of their religion, by which they "glorified God and had power with men." We do not believe that they had an absolute community of goods. The historian does not say so. All the things that were common, were such as were put in the common fund, or distributed in private charity. The owners of the property still retained it under their own control, until they, by their own voluntary act, devoted it to the Lord, and the service of his church. Inspect the narrative, and this will be

manifest. Acts iv. 31-37. Each sold his own land, or other goods, and brought the proceeds, or such portion thereof as he chose, and "laid it down at the Apostle's feet." Joses sold his own land. Ananias and Sapphira sold their possessions. And had they not devoted it to God, they might have kept any part of it, without committing the dreadful sin of lying to the Holy Ghost. Peter acknowledges this, in his address to the man. "While it remained, was it not thine own, and after it was sold, was it not in thine own power?" Their sin was keeping back part of the price, after they had devoted the whole of it to God; and attempting to deceive the Apostles and the Holy Ghost, by concealing the fact, thus violating their vow, and insulting the omniscient Spirit. Their sin was the same with that of Achan, differing only in this: Achan embezzled property devoted or accursed to destruction; they embezzled property that had been devoted to the Lord. Yet whilst the preposterous scheme of a community of goods is not recommended by the example of the primitive church, it is true that such was their liberality, that their common treasury overflowed, "and distribution was made to every man according as he had need." None enjoyed selfishly what his brother lacked, but all comforts and supplies that any possessed were common to all.

5. Our fifth proof is that the first sin committed in the apostolic church, which called for terrible dis-

cipline, was, like the first sin in Paradise, and the first sin after the entrance of the church into Canaan, a sin of covetousness, an act of *unfaithful stewardship*. It was committed in the place of public worship. It was construed to be an insult to the Holy Ghost, being an attempt to pass upon him a lie and a deception, in an act of public worship, for the lie was "not unto men, but unto God."

But omitting, for fear of prolixity, many other Scripture proofs, we proceed to show,

6. That the plan of Christian beneficence practised in the apostolic and the early churches, was ordained by apostolic authority. We mean the plan of depositing in the Lord's treasury, on the first day of the week, an offering proportionate to the prosperity of the offerer. In 1 Cor. xvi. 1, 2, Paul gives directions as follows: "Now concerning the collection for the saints, as I have given order to the churches of Galatia, even so do ye. Upon the first day of the week let every one of you lay by him in store, as God hath prospered him, that there be no gatherings when I come." In the first verse the word translated "given order," is the same that is elsewhere rendered ordained. And the full force of verse second is not brought out in our translation. M'Knight translates it thus, "On the first day of every week, let each one of you lay somewhat by itself, according as he may have prospered, putting it into the treasury, that when I

come there may be no collections." We give the following, which we deem still more literal. "On every first day of the week, let every one of you place by him, (or take with him,) to put into the treasury (literally putting into the treasury) somewhat as he hath been prospered." As *kata ecclesian*, κατὰ ἐκκλησιαν, means every church, Acts xiv. 23, and *kata polin*, κατὰ πόλιν, every city, Acts xv. 21, so *kata mian sabbaton*, κατὰ μίαν σαββάτων, in this passage means every first day of the week. And the reason assigned by the apostles for ordaining this plan: "that there be no collections when I come," shuts us up to the propriety of giving *thesauridzon*, θησαυρίζων, its literal meaning, treasuring up, or putting into a treasury: for, if they had not brought their contributions with them to the treasury, but kept them at home, then there must have been collections, in the churches of Corinth, when he came. The reader will excuse this minute criticism. It is necessary to the true explication of this passage, and we trust it will enable him to perceive, that the following points are here settled by apostolic authority. 1. That the plan of depositing contributions in the Lord's treasury, on the first day of the week, is a good plan. 2. That it was enjoined by the apostle upon quite a number of churches, at least for a time: "as I have ordained in the churches of Galatia, so do ye." 3. That it was *ordained*, or set in order, as a regular system in those churches. Now in reading the Epistle of Paul to these Galatian churches, we find that he gives full instructions to them, in regard to the perpetual duty of stated Christian beneficence: so that there is a strong presumption that the plan which he had set in order amongst them, was to be permanent. And this presumption becomes a certainty, when we remember that what the apostle had ordained in these churches was a part of Christian worship, and had been observed by other churches from the day of Pentecost onward. This collection for the poor saints at Jerusalem, may have been an extraordinary one, but it was to be taken in the ordinary manner.

In the Epistle to the Galatians, the apostle repeatedly presses the duty of Christian beneficence. In ch. ii. 10, he recognizes the duty of remembering the poor. In ch. v. 13, 14, he enforces the golden rule, " by love serve one another—love thy neighbour as thyself." In the last chapter he urges them to " bear one another's burdens, and so fulfil the law of Christ." verse 2. In verses 6–8, he enjoins the support of the ministry, and sharply reproves the niggardly discharge of this duty : " Let him that is taught *communicate,* [κοινωνείτω,] give a part, contribute to him that teacheth, in all good things ;" and in verse 10th, " as we therefore have opportunity, let us work good to all men, especially to them that are of the household of faith." We have, therefore, conclusive proof, that the apostle urged upon the churches of Galatia the doctrines and the duties of Christian stewardship, and that, in the same churches, he had "set in order" the plan of regular Sabbath collections.

And this was no new plan; for God never encouraged his people to "come before him empty." He had always required the homage of the heart, and the "calves of the lips," to be accompanied by the offering of the hand. And when we ponder the foregoing considerations, in connexion with one yet to be stated, viz., that beneficence is a means of grace, we cannot doubt that this religious duty ought to be performed as spiritually, as systematically, and as faithfully as any other; and at least as often as the Sabbath returns.

If these be Scriptural views, if God doth indeed so teach his church in his holy word; then ought the system of "bringing with us, to put into the treasury somewhat, as God hath prospered us" to be restored in the churches. "Thus saith the Lord, Stand ye in the ways, and see, and ask for the old paths, where is the good way, and walk therein, and ye shall find rest for your souls." Jer. vi. 16.

But even if the church will not hearken to the teachings of the Bible, and restore "the old way" of first-day collections, it would undoubtedly be advantageous, if individuals and families would return to this much neglected part of worship.

But before leaving this part of the subject we must not neglect to point out one important feature of the plan ordained by Paul in the churches of Galatia and Corinth, viz., That the contributions were to be made on *every* first day of the week; and that every one was enjoined to give as he had been prospered. The language is explicit: "every one of you." If this precept were obeyed—if every one that professes to love Christ, would bring his offering, and perform systematically this part of worship—then the Lord's treasury would overflow.

CHAPTER X.

Beneficence part of Private and Family Religion.

But whilst we insist that contribution is a part of *public* worship, we would not have it inferred that is not also a part of private and family worship. So far from this, we fully believe that private charity, and family beneficence, are also lovely and appropriate and appointed expressions of the worshipful sentiments of the pious heart.

What does the Spirit, by James, say of the blessed offerings of private charity? "Pure religion and undefiled before God and the Father is this, To visit the fatherless and widows in their affliction, and to keep himself unspotted from the world." James i. 27. In this place, the word which is rendered religion (*threskeia*), θρησκεία, denotes a religious *ceremony*, or the outward form of worship, rather than the inward sentiment. This is the New Testament use of the word; as the reader may satisfy himself by consulting the other places where it is used. *E. g.*, Acts xxvi. 5, "After the straitest sect of our religion, I lived a Pharisee." Here it denotes the Jewish worship. Col. ii. 18. "Let no man beguile you of your reward in the worshipping (*threskeia*) of angels." True, an outward form is not "pure religion before God," unless it proceed from heart-felt piety; but what our apostle here teaches is, that the discharge of the duties of holy charity, is an appropriate expression of gratitude and obedience to God, is a pure and lovely ceremony of our blessed religion. The patriarch Job, in recalling the days when he took delight in religion, "when the candle of God shined upon his head," mentions the discharge of these duties, in a list of the religious observances in which he delighted. "I delivered the poor that cried, and the fatherless, and him that had none to help him, * * * and I caused the widow's heart to sing for joy." Job xxix. 12, 13. "Is not this the fast that I have chosen, * * * * to deal thy bread to the hungry, and that thou bring the poor that are cast out to thy house?" Isai. lviii. 6, 7. And numerous passages, in the teachings of our Lord and his apostles, prove that God ought to be honoured by private and family alms. In the sermon upon the Mount, he gives directions for alms-doing, not only in the synagogue, but in the streets, and enjoins that it be rendered as a religious service to our "Father which seeth in secret."

As we have already stated, when he sent his disciples out to preach, he required them to depend upon private and family hospitality; and he attaches such a *religious* importance to the exercise of this grace, that he declared to his disciples, that it involved, in some cases, the reception or rejection of himself. "He that receiveth you, receiveth me. * * * He that receiveth a prophet in the name of a prophet, shall receive a prophet's reward; and he that receiveth a righteous man in the name of a righteous man, shall receive a righteous man's reward. And whosoever shall give to drink unto one of these little ones, a cup of cold water only, in the name of a disciple, verily, I say unto you, he shall in no wise lose his reward." Matt. x. 40–42.

Indeed we have more frequent directions about private and family beneficence than we have about private and family prayer; and we have as much reason to suppose, that there is no prayer to be offered except public prayer, as that there are to be no alms done except public alms. The above and many other passages also prove, that it is not only an office of our religion, but one of the most important means of grace, even a means whereby, often, Christ and He that sent him are received: and whereby "the righteous man's reward" is obtained. Even the smallest act of charity done as an act of spiritual worship—"in the name of a disciple"—"as to the Lord and not to men," shall in no wise lose its reward.

It is in the secrecy of the individual bosom, and in the domestic sanctuary, that the elements of holy charity can be most efficiently cultivated. Indeed, there is a truth in the often-perverted maxim,

"Charity must begin at home." If parents would cherish the alms-doing graces in their closets, and by private deeds of beneficence; and if they would make the inculcation of the doctrines, and the exercise of the duties of Christian beneficence, a part of family worship, we have no doubt that the results to themselves, to their households, and to the church of God, would be most glorious. This might be done with great profit and propriety on the first day of the week. It is of all days the most suitable for alms-deeds. Its weekly return reminds us of creation, providence, and redemption. Originally appointed to commemorate the great fact that Jehovah created the world, and the great doctrine that he is "possessor of heaven and of earth," it was changed to the first day of the week to commemorate the completion of a new creation, by the resurrection of Christ, the redemption of the world by his blood; and the doctrine that "we are not our own, but bought with a price, and therefore bound to glorify God with our bodies and spirits which are God's." How well calculated is it, then, to remind us, that God is our sovereign Creator and Redeemer, that all we have was given by him, and that to his glory we should employ it! How well adapted to awaken our gratitude, by its inspiring associations; and how distinctly does the silent language of its dawning light whisper to the believer's heart, "to do good and to communicate forget not, for with such sacrifices God is well pleased!" Heb. xiii. 16. Let the parents and the children, therefore, gather around the family altar on the Sabbath morning; let the fact that it is "the Lord's day," remind them that they, and all they have are the Lord's; let some story of a Saviour's beneficence be read, some doctrine of gratitude and self-denial taught, some song of thanksgiving sung, a prayer resembling the Lord's own prayer offered, and then let "*every one* place by him, to put into the treasury, somewhat as he hath been prospered," either by success or self-denial; and from the domestic to the public sanctuary will flow a pure and blessed rill of living waters, to swell the tide of that "river, the streams whereof shall make glad the city of God!" And back into the bosom of that family will flow, with a current peaceful as the Sabbath, and sparkling as the dew of heaven, the perennial waters of blessedness. "He that watereth shall be watered also himself!"

Such, as the writer believes, are the Scripture principles, and such is the Scripture plan of Christian beneficence: and in our next chapter we propose succinctly to set forth its advantages.

CHAPTER XI.

Advantages of the Scripture Plan of Beneficence.

1. It brings the duty of alms-giving before the conscience with all the solemnity and tenderness of a religious claim. It exhibits it constantly as a part of the worship of God, which we may not omit without sin. And when a man feels that the duty, industriously to acquire property with a view to honour the Lord with it, is a *religious* duty, and that to offer a part of what he acquires to the Lord, is a part of Christian *worship*, which he has no more right to neglect, than he has to neglect prayer, praise, the Sabbath, or the sacraments, he will be both more industrious and more liberal.

2. Many would be willing to give a *little at a time*, and that *frequently*, who might be tempted to withhold the aggragate of those littles, if demanded all at once. An aggregate amount presents a larger bait, a stronger temptation to our innate covetousness, than do the several smaller sums of which it is composed. Hence,

3. More will be cast into the Lord's treasury by this systematic method of collection.

4. The plan has the sanction of *Divine analogy*. *God aggregates by littles!* He replenishes the earth and the springs of water, not by waterspouts, but by drops. He forms globes of grains of sand. He fills the ocean from the mountain rills. He forms the mighty oak from the acorn. He erects his kingdom from beginnings small as the germ of the mustard seed. He thus teaches us the *power of the littles!* And the church must humble herself to learn more of the power of the littles, before she can achieve her grand triumph!

5. The other exercises of worship, on the Lord's day, fit the mind for the duty of alms-doing, and by a reflex influence, the act of charity fosters the graces of the heart.

6. The plan of giving "on every first day of the week," would most effectually tend to restore the habit of giving from *principle* and not from *impulse*. The most perennial springs are the least liable to floods. The heart that dictates charity from steadfast principle, and performs it as a regular weekly religious duty, will be little liable to be betrayed, under some exciting appeal, into those impulsive and extravagant gifts, which may be followed with regrets, and which, like the torrent in the desert, leave the channel of benevolence torn and dry. But,

7. If it be the Bible plan, as we trust has been proven: if it be God's plan, and if beneficence be indeed part of every Sabbath's worship, we are

bound to adopt the plan, even if we could perceive none of its peculiar advantages. If it is a divinely recommended system, God will bless it, and will demonstrate by its success, that after all, "the foolishness of God is wiser than men!"

CHAPTER XII.

Systematic Beneficence a Means of Grace and Evangelization.

The Divine Being ordinarily accomplishes his purposes by means, both in the spiritual and material world: and our ignorance of the mode of their operation, is no valid objection to the doctrine of means. It were folly to say, "I do not know how God employs gravitation as a means of preserving the balance, and perpetuating the motions of the planetary system, and therefore I will not believe that he does it." And it were equal folly to say, "I do not know *how* spirit influences spirit through means, and therefore I will not believe it possible." Our ignorance of the *mode* in which the universal Governor works by means, should not shake our belief in the fact: whilst if we can to any extent understand the adaptedness of means to their end, it may prove an additional encouragement to use them.

The term grace, in the Scriptures, generally denotes favour shown to the undeserving. But as saving favour is conferred upon men, through the efficacious working of the Holy Spirit, the term is sometimes employed to denote that working; or in other words, that influence exerted by the Spirit of God upon the spirit of man, whereby he "worketh in him both to will and to do of his good pleasure." To deny that such an influence is exerted, were as unphilosophical as infidel, for such denial would be in the face of facts. That spirit does influence spirit is a thing of which we are every day both conscious and observant. The effect of eloquence, poetry, or song, are the result of mind operating upon mind. The eloquence, the poetry, the song, is but a means, a material means; mind-spirit is the living agent. And if one created spirit may thus influence another, is it not absurd to deny, that the uncreated "Father of spirits" can influence the minds which he has made? Is it not irrational to suppose that he would withdraw all control from them?

Now in both senses of the term grace, it is true that the belief of the doctrines, and the practice of the duties of Christian beneficence are *means of grace.*

I. The faithful excercise of stewardship is a means through which the favour of God in temporal things is conferred. To this effect the language of Divine promise is explicit: "Honour the Lord with thy substance, and with the first fruits of all thine increase; *so* shall thy barns be filled with plenty, and thy presses shall gush forth with new wine." "He that hath pity upon the poor lendeth unto the Lord, and that which he hath given will he pay him again." Prov. iii. 9, 10; and xix. 17.

To the church and nation of Israel were given ample promises of temporal blessing, if they would prove faithful to the stewardship committed to them. And when obedient, they realized to the full these promises. See Lev. xxvi. 3-5; Deut. xxviii. 1-15; Ps. xli. 1-3. Peerless prosperity attended them, when they kept the ordinances of God, which, as we have seen, largely consisted in offerings of property to his honour. And when we consider that the history of Israel is the history of a divine administration, in which the principles of God's government are illustrated, for the instruction of the world, we will feel bound to take that history as written for our warning and encouragement. One subordinate sense, in which all the nations of the earth are to be blessed in Abraham and his seed, is that the rich and varied instruction furnished by the history of God's dealings with them will prove of inestimable value to the nations. And he who will study that history, will be surprised to find how fully our doctrine is established by it. It is impossible to account for the wonderful facts presented in the history of Judea, without admitting, that there is a degree of efficiency in the principle we are advocating, which has never yet been adequately appreciated. How can we account for the fact that such amazing masses of population as occupied Judea in the palmy days of Israel, were not only subsisted, but rolled in abundance: whilst in times of Israel's religious degeneracy, their prosperity departed; and at the present day the country will hardly subsist its sparse and wretched population. We can only account for the facts, by admitting, that faithful stewardship is a means of temporal prosperity, and that there is a depth of meaning yet unsounded, in the declaration of Jehovah by the latest of her prophets, "Bring ye all the tithes into the storehouse, that there may be meat in my house, and prove me now herewith, saith the Lord of hosts, if I will not open you the windows of heaven, and pour you out a blessing that there shall not be room enough to receive it. And I will rebuke the devourer, for your sakes, and he shall not destroy the fruits of your ground; neither shall your vine cast her fruit before the time in the field, saith the Lord of hosts. And all nations shall call you blessed; for ye shall be a delightsome land, saith the Lord of hosts." Mal. iii. 10–12. Unexampled prosperity was bestowed upon God's people whilst obedient; whilst a curse proportionately heavy fell upon them, when unfaithful to their high trust.

Let the Christian reader rest assured, then, that "there is that *scattereth* and yet *increaseth;* and there is that *withholdeth* more than is meet, but it *tendeth to poverty!* The liberal soul shall be made fat, and he that watereth shall be watered also himself." Prov. xi. 24, 25. "The liberal deviseth liberal things; and by liberal things shall he stand." Isa. xxxii. 8. Let him remember that "he that giveth unto the poor shall not lack, but he that hideth his eyes shall have many a curse," Prov. xxviii. 27; that Jesus hath said, "there is no man that hath left house * * * or lands for my sake and the gospel's; but he shall receive an hundred fold now in this time, houses and lands with persecutions; and in the world to come eternal life." Mark x. 29, 30.

With such passages of God's word before them, it is amazing that Christian men hesitate to believe that it is for their temporal advantage to devise liberal things. The most profitable investment, which a man can make, of a portion of his worldly estate, is to lend it to the Lord, for the comfort of his saints, for the spread of the gospel, and for the support of the poor, and the salvation of the perishing heathen. In the passage quoted above from Prov. xix. 17, the Lord condescends to say, that he will consider money bestowed in beneficence as a *loan* to himself, and he gives his promissory note for the repayment. And he is the best security in the universe! Capitalists are always ready to make a profitable investment; and are eager to take stock in any new institution, which they suppose to be safe and profitable; and for this they are willing to take reasonable assurances even from men: but when their Maker gives them the assurance that a portion of their funds will be both safe and profitable in his hands, and pledges himself to repay them again, they hesitate, demur, and sometimes not only refuse, but get angry with the agent of God who would negotiate the loan. Like the first parents of our race, we are too apt to distrust God's method of promoting our temporal welfare, and rely upon our own: and, grasping at God's share, lose both that and our own. Is it a wonder that he often makes men feel their dependence upon him for all their capital, and for their power to get wealth, by permitting disasters to befal their business?

Besides being a means of procuring temporal blessing, we ought here to remark, that Christian beneficence enables those, who practise it, to *enjoy* the life that now is. There is a positive enjoyment in doing good. The exercise of the benevolent affections is itself delightful, and imparts a zest to the rational pursuits and pleasures of life. "Remember the words of the Lord Jesus, how he said, it is more blessed to give than to receive." Acts xx. 35.

II. Systematic beneficence is a means of spiritual grace.

1. It is repeatedly called *a grace* in Scripture. The Apostle Paul, in his second letter to the Corinthians, stimulates them to liberality in their gifts by the example of the Macedonians, and uses this language, "Moreover, brethren, we do you to wit of the grace of God bestowed upon the churches of

Macedonia; how that, in a great trial of affliction, the abundance of their joy and their deep poverty abounded unto the riches of their liberality." 2 Cor. viii. 1–6. He calls the disposition to be liberal, in their straitened circumstances, *a grace* bestowed on them of God; both because it was a fruit of God's Spirit working in their hearts, (efficient grace,) and because the disposition itself was a blessing (a favour) and a means of their spiritual advancement. In verse seven, he uses this language, "See that ye abound in this grace also," in which he ranks the grace of liberality with those of faith, utterance, knowledge, and love. In verse eight, he points out one of the advantages of this grace, viz., that it "proves the sincerity of our love;" and in verse nine, he mentions the grace of Christ, as at once the foundation and the motive of the grace of liberality in Christians. "For ye know the grace of our Lord Jesus Christ, that though he was rich, yet for your sakes he became poor, that ye, through his poverty might be rich."

In 2 Cor. ix. 14, Christian beneficence is spoken of as "the exceeding grace of God in you." Peter likewise, in exhorting believers to practise hospitality, says, "As every man hath received the gift, (favour or endowment,) even so minister the same one to another, as good stewards of the manifold *grace* of God," in which he teaches that the disposition to minister to the comfort of others is a grace of God. Proofs might be multiplied, but it is needless.

2. A disposition and ability to be actively benevolent, are favours bestowed by God; and beneficence itself is the means of procuring and fostering other graces. Even if we could discover in the exercises of charity no adaptedness to produce such results, we are obliged to believe, on the authority of God's word, that they will promote the spiritual good of those who practise them. But, if we mistake not, there is an obvious beauty and fitness in the mode of operation of this grace.

"Ye have the poor with you always, and whensoever ye will ye may do them good," said our Lord to his disciples. And the fact here stated is probably one that is to continue so long as the church is in her militant state. It becomes a question of intense interest, " *Why* has God so constituted human society? Why does he put down one and raise another up?" Why does he, in his providence, leave some destitute of this world's goods, whilst others have all that heart can wish? Why do some dwell in the region and shadow of death, whilst others bask beneath the full splendours of the Sun of Righteousness? Why not make all men equal, in point of worldly goods, and civil liberty, and religious privileges? Doubtless one object of this mysterious arrangement is, to afford opportunity for the exercise and culture of the benevolent affections of our nature. If all were equal, in point of worldly condition and spiritual privilege, there would be no place for "communication," no room for the exercise of those kind offices which call forth the nobler feelings of humanity. The economy of the divine Being, in the distribution of the comforts which are needful to the body and the soul, resembles that which he has adapted to the distribution of that element, so necessary to life, which teems from the clouds, and rolls in the ocean. If the earth were a dead level, *circulation* would stop, universal stagnation and pestilence and death would ensue. The water is not equally distributed, and yet by circulation its end is better promoted, than if it were. The ocean, the lake, the river, are rich in watery stores, but they are not penurious. The ocean's mighty bosom, warmed by the genial rays of the sun, gives liberally of his treasure to the clouds. The lakes and seas and rivers add their bounty. The clouds shower down the charity, of which they are the bearers, upon the thirsty plain, and mountain, and valley, reviving and cheering the bosom of nature. But are the ocean, the sea, the lake, the mighty river, impoverished by their continual giving? Far from it. The earth, grateful for the favour it has received, pours back the water, purified, and laden with that which will bless the inhabitants of the waters, into the purling rivulets. The rivulets pay their contributions to the larger streams and mighty rivers, and they hasten to pour their majestic waters into the lake, the sea, or the ocean, assured that giving doth not impoverish. It is thus in the economy of Christian beneficence. The Creator requires those to whom he has given abundance, to *put it in circulation;* assuring them that it will return to them again, if given from proper motives. The pious bosom, warmed by the genial beams of the Sun of Righteousness, sends forth the kindly exhalations of Christian charity. They descend in refreshing showers upon the poor and distressed, the ignorant, the guilty, and the lost. They are blessed, comforted, converted, it may be, unto God. Their prayers ascend for their benefactor, while the alms of the benefactor themselves "come up for a remembrance before God." The streams of Divine favour begin to flow back to him, they enlarge, grow deeper and wider, and pour blessings upon him in this life: yea, they roll on,

> "Until he bathes his gladdened soul
> In seas of heavenly rest."

3. Christian beneficence is the means by which the God of grace developes, in the believer's soul, the principles of the new life, and produces in his heart and conduct the fruits of the Spirit. The healthy development of the powers of the soul, like that of the body, depends upon right exercise. The child, that is reared in total inactivity, will grow imbecile and sickly. The mind whose powers are not called into exercise, will remain weak, and will

most likely become morbid. And it would be contrary to the analogy of the Divine operations, to expect that the new spiritual life, begun in the soul by regeneration, can be carried forward, in a healthy and proportionate expansion, without the proper *exercise* of its various functions. The babe in Christ can never "come unto a perfect man, unto the measure of the stature of the fulness of Christ" without the due exercise of his renovated powers.

Now all these powers are called into healthful and invigorating play, in the faithful discharge of the duties of a Christian stewardship. Its aim is the glory of God in the salvation of a world! Its principles are based upon sovereign and immutable justice! Its motive is supreme love to God, and equal love to our neighbour, love kindled at love's own fountain, love lighted at the cross! Its rule is the will of the Holy One! Its "fruits, love, joy, peace, long-suffering, gentleness, goodness, faith, meekness, temperance!" Its duties require the exercise of "the same mind that was also in Christ Jesus," and call to the imitation of his perfect example. Like him, the good steward must practise self-denial, and be willing to give his substance, and himself, if need be, for the good of others. Like him he must be humble, compassionate, forgiving, and disposed to suffer even for enemies. Like him he must esteem it his "meat to do his Father's will and finish his work." And is it not obvious, that the practice of Christian beneficence thus cultivates the very temper of Heaven, and is the very process by which the soul is fitted for that blessed abode?

4. Christian liberality is a means by which "they that are Christ's, crucify the flesh with the affections and lusts." *Covetousness*, as it was an element of the first sin of the human mind, so is it still one of the most deceitful and dangerous. From the hour in which it first seized upon the heart in Paradise, on through the whole of man's sad history, it has been an ever-living, ever-gnawing worm, that has eaten at the vitals of his peace. "Covetousness is idolatry." Col. iii. 5. "The covetous man is an idolater," Eph. v. 5, because he turns from the Creator, and seeks in created things that protection, that portion, that pleasure, which can be found only in God. The man, who loves and trusts in riches or any created good, more than in the uncreated Fountain of fulness, makes a god of the creature, attributes to it divine power, reposes in it that confidence which should only be placed in God, or at least it esteems the maker less than the thing made. Covetousness took possession of our first parents' hearts when they turned from God to the creature, preferred the forbidden fruit to his favour, and trusted in a devil's lure, rather than in a Divine promise. It is, therefore, the sin which most obstinately retains the heart as an idol's temple, to the exclusion of the true God, who should

be there enthroned. Hence it is peculiarly God-dishonouring, dangerous, and damning.

Covetousness is the prolific parent of all our sins. As idolatry, it is a violation of the first three precepts of the decalogue; as unlawful desire it leads to the breach of all the other six; and, therefore, the closing precept of that wonderful law strikes at the root of all evil, by the injunction, "Thou shalt not covet." And Christ said to his disciples, "Take heed and beware of covetousness." Luke xii. 15. Well did the Apostle [1 Tim. vi. 10] declare, "The love of money is the root of all these evils, which while some coveted after, they have erred from the faith, and pierced themselves through with many sorrows. But thou, O man of God, flee these things."

It is the tendency of covetousness, perhaps more than of any other sin, to strengthen its sway over the heart, and wax worse and worse. Other desires of the flesh may fail, with the natural decline of our powers; but this, unless eradicated, grows with our years and becomes more intense by repeated indulgence. Such is the testimony of universal experience, and such is the teaching of him who made man, and "knoweth what is in man." Of the avaricious man he saith, "there is no end of all his labour, neither is his eye satisfied with riches—he that loveth silver shall not be satisfied with silver, nor he that loveth abundance with increase. The abundance of the rich will not suffer him to sleep."

Ecc. "Hell and destruction are not full, so the eyes of man are never satisfied." Prov. xxvii. 20. If, then, covetousness be a sin so heinous in God's sight, a sin that tends so completely to banish God from the heart; if it be the root of many other evils; if its native tendency is to strengthen as men advance in life, it is a most "deceitful lust," a most dangerous foe to grace; and the means that will tend to crucify this lust, to eradicate this root of bitterness, to make this Dagon fall down before the ark of God, ought surely to be hailed with joy by every professed believer, and diligently used as a means of salvation. And what can prove a more efficacious means of accomplishing this, than the belief of the doctrines and the practice of the duties of Christian stewardship. The faithful steward of Christ believes God's word. He believes that God is the creator and sovereign of all things, and that they should be employed for his glory. He believes that Christ hath redeemed sinners, and that the redeemed are not their own, and are therefore bound to glorify God with their bodies and spirits which are God's. He goes to the cross, and there "the love of Christ constraineth him" to live to Christ. And thus sweetly constrained by "bonds of love," he presents himself and all his resources a cheerful sacrifice to God. Feeling that he owes all to Christ, he surrenders all to him, and resolves, as a faithful servant, to "occupy till his Lord come." And he is "not slothful in business, fervent in spirit, serving the Lord." If in secular employment, the love of Christ warms his heart and nerves his arm. By honourable industry he aims to acquire property, not that he may hoard it, or consume it upon his lusts, but that he may have wherewith to honour the Lord. God and not gold is his chief end. And like his Divine Master he can, in some measure, affirm, " My meat is to do the will of him that sent me!"

Even then, in desiring wealth, the good steward's love is not bestowed upon money, but upon the God in whose service he wishes to employ it. His life is that of an affectionate child labouring for a good father. His toil is sweetened by the anticipation of the good which he aims to accomplish. Piety is carried into business; business becomes a part of piety. " He uses this world as not abusing it." Now is it not manifest, that such principles and such a practice tend directly to put to death the sin of covetousness. They take away its very food; before money can become an idol, it is offered in spiritual sacrifice to the true God. Every act of heart-born charity drives a nail in the very vitals of this lust, and fastens it more firmly to its cross. And as the practice of systematic beneficence grows into a habit, "the old man, which is corrupt, after the deceitful lusts, is put off," the good steward is " renewed in the spirit of his mind, and puts on the new man," which after God is created in righteousness and true holiness." Under the renewing power of the divine Spirit, such is the legitimate tendency of Christian charity.

And as of covetousness, so of all the brood of "deceitful lusts" of which it is the parent; they are banished from the heart and life of the believer, by the Holy Spirit, through the counteracting instrumentality of the grace of beneficence.

CHAPTER XIII.

Oblation a Means of Grace—Illustrated from the Mosaic Economy.

And the foregoing view of the subject receives much illustration and force, from an inspection of the design and tendencies of the Mosaic system of offerings; as would appear had we space for such inspection. A point or two is all we can suggest.

One great object of the Jewish ceremonial, was so to employ the people of Israel, in duties of religion, as to restrain them from idolatry. It aimed to accomplish this object by giving them full religious occupation, by the burdensome ritual, which demanded so much of their time and substance, as to leave them little or no opportunity for them to go after the gods of the other nations. It also required them to sacrifice many of those things which the Gentiles worshipped as gods. In Egypt, where Israel had been in bondage, and in other neighbouring nations, cattle and other animals were worshipped; also, gods of silver and gold. Israel was commanded to sacrifice to the true God cattle and sheep and goats and certain birds; and to offer gold and silver and other property to the service of religion and the support of the poor. Now since "covetousness"—the love of property for its own sake or for selfish ends—"is idolatry;" since it was the first form of idolatry in Paradise, and is the world-pervading form of that sin, we cannot doubt that one object of the very expensive system of offerings, which was imposed upon Israel, was to constrain them to offer to the true God, what they were so much in danger of idolizing. We are far from saying that this was the chief design of that economy; but this was one design, and we can see an admirable adaptedness of the means to the end. The habit of offering property to the service of the true God, was well calculated to prevent them from making an idol of it. Nor should we fail, in this connection, to note the sad yet striking fact, that the apostasy of Israel, in the days of Malachi, was occasioned by a covetous attempt to defeat the end of this system. "They robbed God in tithes and offerings, and were cursed with a curse." Mal. iii. 8. And alas! in their long rejection, they continue to be perhaps the most covetous race on earth. Let the Christian church be warned by the awful doom of Israel to "take heed and beware of covetousness, which is idolatry."

Christian beneficence is a means of grace whereby "the lusts of the flesh, the lust of the eye, and the pride of life" may be mortified.

5. It is a means of *laying up treasure in heaven.* Upon this we need not enlarge. The Bible is explicit. "Your Father who seeth in secret shall reward you openly." "Sell that ye have and give alms: provide yourselves bags which wax not old, a treasure in the heavens that faileth not." "Sell all that thou hast and distribute to the poor, and thou shalt have treasure in heaven."

6. *Christian beneficence* is not only one of the graces by which we are to obtain evidence of our union to Christ, and of our personal justification, but it will be mentioned on the judgment day, as the evidence of our justification! See Matt. xxv. 31–46. We say it will then be appealed to, not as the meritorious *ground,* but as the *evidence* of our union to Christ and our justification by faith in him. "Come unto me, ye blessed of my Father, inherit the kingdom, prepared for you from the foundation of the world!" Why? "For I was an hungered, and ye gave me meat." Surprised at this, the righteous ask, "When saw we *thee* an hungered and fed thee? or thirsty and gave thee drink?" "And the King shall answer and say unto them, Verily, I say unto you, inasmuch as ye have done it unto one of the least of these my brethren, ye have done it unto me!" Compassionate Lord! Wondrous condescension! To identify thyself with the humblest of thy poor, yet ransomed ones! To take them into such close union with thy glorious self, as to consider kindness shown to them as kindness

shown to thyself; and neglect of them as neglect of thee!

And ah! how terribly will the avaricious be made to feel, upon that awful day, the folly and criminality of their covetousness: "Depart, ye cursed!" Why? "Because ye had no part in me, as was proved by the fact that 'I was an hungred and ye gave me no meat, I was thirsty and ye gave me no drink, I was a stranger and ye took me not in, naked and ye clothed me not, sick and in prison and ye visited me not.'" "Then shall they answer him saying, Lord, when saw we *thee* an hungered or athirst, or a stranger or naked or sick or in prison, and did not minister unto thee? Then shall he answer them saying, Verily, I say unto you, inasmuch as *ye did it not* unto one of the least of these, ye did it not to me. And these shall go away into everlasting punishment, but the righteous into life eternal."

7. Lastly: systematic beneficence is an essential *means* of *evangelization*. This needs no proof, except a reference to the Bible, and to our previous discussion. "How shall they call upon him, in whom they have not believed? and how shall they believe in him of whom they have not heard? and how shall they hear without a preacher? and how shall they preach except they be sent?" Rom. x. 14. And how shall they be sent without the pecuniary means? "For no man goeth a warfare at his own charges." But having estab-

lished the position, that the faithful stewardship of God's people constituted the instrumentality by which the gospel was to be spread abroad, we deem it unnecessary to enlarge farther upon this topic.

CONCLUDING APPEAL.

HAVE we succeeded, dear reader, in producing in your mind the conviction that the views embodied in this treatise are true? Have we proven that Christian stewardship as systematic beneficence is an essential element of Christianity? That its principles belong to the *faith*, its duties to the *practice*, of the true Christian? That it is part of religious *worship?* That it is an important means of grace and evangelization? Are you convinced that it is the element of our holy religion, upon which, in a large measure, depend the sanctification of God's children, the propagation of the gospel, the triumph of the church, and the manifestation of the glory of God?

We have drawn all our proofs from holy Scripture and authentic history. It has been our aim to let God's own word plead his own cause upon these pages. Are you convinced that these positions are true? Then have you no more right to neglect gospel beneficence, than you have to neglect praise, prayer, preaching, the Sabbath, the sacraments or any other duty of religion. You are under solemn obligations to adopt yourself, and to promote in the church, the scriptural principles and the scriptural plan of beneficence, and to do *your share*, whatever that may be, to secure "Glory to God in the highest, on earth peace, good will toward men!"

READER, may God give you grace to be a faithful and good steward of all that has been entrusted to you: and at last, when our Lord shall come to reckon with his servants, may you receive the cheering plaudit, "Well done, good and faithful servant, thou hast been faithful over a few things, I will make thee ruler over many things, ENTER THOU INTO THE JOY OF THY LORD!"

INDEX OF SUBJECTS.

	PAGE
ABILITY, The measure of giving,	46
ABEL'S offering,	51
ABRAHAM'S offering,	52
ACHAN. Sin of	79
ADVANTAGES of Scripture system	90
ANANIAS and Sapphira, Sin of	79
ANALOGY of faith, Important	12
ANNIVERSARIES a snare,	49
ASSIMILATING tendency of the Gospel.	17
APPEAL, Concluding	114
BENEFICENCE, SYSTEMATIC	
An essential element of Christianity,	16 17
A part of practical piety,	14
An imitation of Christ,	103
A part of public worship,	63
" " private and family worship,	85
Its motive, love,	37 41
Must be cheerful,	47
" " constant,	47
" " diligent,	44
" " proportionate to ability,.	46
" " unostentatious,	47
Means of crucifying flesh,	104
" developing the graces,	102
" of temporal benefits,	94
" of grace,	93 98
" of evangelization,	112
" of laying up treasures in heaven,	111
" of temporal enjoyment	98
Will be mentioned at the judgment,	111
BODY of Christ anointed,	69
CALVIN on Acts ii. 42,	74
CALL, Every man should have a	43
How ascertained,	44
CEREMONIAL system rational.	
CHARITY called religion,	85
Must begin at home,	88
CHARTER of the church,	52
CHRISTIANITY a system,	9
Contains the elements of prosperity and extension,	15
Not a dead organism,	11
CHURCH, same under both dispensations,	57
COMMUNICATION part of worship	70
A New Testament sacrifice,	73
COMMUNITY of goods inexpedient	78 79

	PAGE
COVENANT of grace a sovereign act,	30
Of works what tested in,	27
COVETOUSNESS the first sin,	28
Is idolatry,	104
Is dangerous and heinous,	105
The antidote to,	106
DEACONS,	56 74 77
DEED of trust, God's word a	25
DISPENSATION explained,	60
Change of, What meant by	60
DISSEMINATION an essential of religion.	15
ECONOMY explained,	60
EDEN, Economy of	27
ELECTION, how made sure,	21
ESSENTIAL and non-essential, Man not the judge of	12
EVANGELIZATION the church's work,	16
FEAR as a motive,	39
FIRST-DAY COLLECTIONS of Apostolic order,	80
To be perpetual,	82
FORFEITURE of rights by the fall	30
FOUNDATION of moral obligation	26
Of stewardship,	27
FRUIT of a system, its seed,	15
FRUITS of the spirit,	21
GIVING a grace,	25 99 100
A part of worship,	22 51 71
Doth not impoverish,	102
GLORY defined,	37
GOVERNMENT a divine ordinance	35
GRACE. Definition of	93
Oblation a	99 100
Oblation a means of	93 98
HEBREWS xiii. 16 explained,	73
HOME-BENEFICENCE, Benefit of	88
INEQUALITY of wealth, Design of	100
INVESTMENTS, The best	97
INVESTITURE of Noah,	31
ISRAEL'S history illustrative,	95
JACOB'S vow,	52
JUDAS. Sin of	67 68
KINGDOM of heaven defined,	17
LAW. Every one of God's binding till repealed,	59
LEAVEN, parable of explained,	17
LITTLES. The power of	91
LORD PARAMOUNT, God the	27
LORD's prayer teaches beneficence,	22

117

INDEX OF SUBJECTS.

	PAGE
LOVE the motive to duty,	33 41
MARY'S box of ointment,	68
MEANS, Doctrine of	93
MOSAIC ECONOMY, Design of	109
Antidote to idolatry	110
Its morality still obligatory,	58
Illustrations from	109
MOTIVES, Doctrine of	33 39
MUSTARD SEED, Lessons of	15 18
NOAH'S offering,	52
OBLATION an expression of piety	55
Duty of not abolished,	59
In the first family,	51
Inseparable from the ancient worship,	57
Means of grace illustrated from Mosaic economy,	109
The first act of N. Testament worship,	66
OBLIGATION, Moral grounds of	26 31
Not relaxed by the gospel,	34
Perpetual,	58
"OCCUPY till I come," explained	44
OLD TESTAMENT dispensation, in what sense abolished,	58
OSTENTATION to be avoided,	42
PENTECOST, Lessons of	70
PLAN OF BENEFICENCE, Scripture,	50 51
Advantages of	90
Permanent,	82
Ordained by apostolic authority,	80
PREACHING, Defective	13
PROPERTY, Basis of	34
Duty to acquire,	90
Power to gain is of God,	35
To be used for God's glory,	38
RELIGION, Spirit of immutable	59
James' definition of	85
"RETIRING from business," is it right?	45
RITUAL LAW a system of beneficence,	55
Quoted as such by Paul,	65
Its spirit perpetual,	65
SABBATH collections ordained,	80 82
Best day for beneficence,	88
Lessons of "	88 89
SACRIFICES, their language,	55
New Testament,	65
SEED of a system, its fruit,	15
SECRECY in giving not obligatory	48
SELF-GRATULATION to be avoided	48
SOVEREIGNTY OF GOD basis of obligation,	26
In the covenant of works,	27
In the covenant of grace,	30

	PAGE
SOVEREIGNTY OF GOD basis of obligation,	26
In Noachic, Abrahamic, and Mosaic covenants,	31
In the system of offerings,	32
In the gospel,	32
SPIRIT OF GOD, author of life, light, and order,	10
His energy essential to Christianity,	11
STEWARD, an ancient office,	24
Definition of	24
Every man a	26
The good described,	106
STEWARDSHIP, Theory of	24
Much neglected,	16
Fruit and seed of Christianity	16
Of the church changed,	60
Foundation of	26
A condition of innocence,	28
How affected by the fall,	26 30
Sin to fail in	34
Motives and end of	37 41
Is an antidote to covetousness,	106
Results of, to the faithful,	94
Rule of	43
Taught in Eden,	25
STEWARDSHIP, doctrine of proved by Old Testament prophecies,	64
The first act of New Testament worship,	66
The examples of Christ,	66
The precepts of Christ,	66 68
The teaching of apostles,	69
The testimony of the Fathers	75
SYNAGOGUE, Oblation part of worship of	56
Worship the model of Christian worship,	74
TABERNACLE, Illustration from	12
TALENTS, Parable of explained,	44
TITHES,	38 53
TITLES TO PROPERTY, Origin of	34
TESTIMONY of the fathers,	56 75 76
UNFAITHFULNESS IN STEWARDSHIP the first sin,	28
The sin of Judas,	68
WATER, Illustration from	101
WITNESS of the Spirit,	20
WORSHIP defined,	54
Partly consists in oblation,	22 57
Material media necessary in	54
Spirit of, ever the same,	57
Of the apostolic church, described,	70

TEXTS OF SCRIPTURE,

QUOTED AND ILLUSTRATED IN THE PRECEDING TREATISE.

	PAGE
Gen. i. 26,	34
" ii. 8–17,	27
" iv. 3,	51
" vii. 20,	52
" viii. 20,	52
" ix. 1–17,	31 34
" xii. 3,	31 52
" xiv. 20,	52
" xxii.,	31
" xxii. 18,	53
" xxvi. 4,	53
" xxviii. 22,	52
Exod xx. 2,	31
" xxiii. 15,	55
" xxxiv. 20,	56
Lev. xix. 9, 10,	32
" xxiii 22,	32
" xxvii. 30–32,	53
Deut. viii. 17, 18,	38
" x. 14,	28
" xv. 7, 8,	56
" xvi. 10,	47
" xvi. 16,	55
1 Sam. ii. 7,	35
Job xxix. 12, 13,	86
Ps. xxiv. 1,	28
" lxxv. 7,	35
" clxi. 2,	65
Prov. iii. 9,	19 38 94
" ix. 2,	75
" xi. 24, 25,	89 96
" xvi. 4,	37
" xix. 17,	94 97
" xxviii. 27,	97
" xxvii. 20,	106
Eccl. iv. 8,	105
" v. 10, 12,	105
Isa. xxx. 21,	44
" xxxii. 8,	97
" xiii. 1,	70
" lx.,	64
Jer. vi. 16,	83
Dan. iv. 35,	35
Hag. ii. 8,	29
Zech. xiv. 14,	64
Mal. i. 11,	64

	PAGE
Mal. iii. 10–12,	96
Matt. iii. 18,	70
" v. 4,	111
" v. 16,	48
" vi 1, 2,	42
" vi. 3,	47 57
" vi. 1–18,	66
" vii. 12,	19
" ix. 38,	19
" x. 40, 42,	87
" xiii. 31–33,	17
" xvi. 24,	21
" xix. 19,	19
" xxv. 15,	46
" xxv. 14–30,	25
" xxv. 31–46,	111
Mark iv. 31, 32,	17
" x. 29, 30,	97
" xiv. 1–9,	68 69
" xvi. 15,	19
Luke x. 2,	19
" x. 7,	68
" xii. 16–21,	45
" xii. 21,	46
" xii. 33,	111
" xii. 15,	105
" xii. 48,	46
" xiii. 19, 21,	19
" xviii. 22,	111
John xii 6,	67
" xii. 3–8,	68
" xiii. 29,	67
Acts ii. 42,	70
" ii. 44, 45,	78
" iv. 32, 37,	78
" v. 4,	79
" vi. 4,	78
" xx. 28,	33
" xx 35,	98
Rom. viii. 2,	11
" viii. 15,	40
" viii. 16,	20
" viii. 9,	21
" viii. 7,	40
" x. 14,	19 112
" xi. 26,	37

	PAGE
Rom. xii. 11,	106
" xiv. 7–9,	33
" xv. 26,	72
1 Cor. iii. 8,	11
" iv. 1,	25
" vi. 19, 20,	33 38
" ix. 9–14,	65
" x. 31,	38
" xiv. 4,	49
" xiii. 3,	41
" xvi. 2,	45
" xvi. 1, 2,	80
2 Cor. v. 14,	40
" viii. 9,	21
" viii. 12,	46 47
" viii 4,	72
" viii. 1–6,	99
" ix. 2–13,	38 47 72
" ix. 14,	99
Gal. v. 6,	41
" v. 13,	61
" v. 22,	21
Eph. i. 10,	10
" i. 11,	85
" ii. 22,	12
" iii. 10,	11
" iv. 15, 16,	13
" iv. 24,	107
" v. 5,	104
Phil. ii. 5–8,	21
" iv. 15,	72
Col. iii. 5,	104
1 Tim. vi. 17, 18,	73
" vi. 10,	105
2 Tim i. 7,	39
" iii. 16, 17,	50
Tit. i. 7,	25
James i. 27,	85
1 Pet. iv. 10,	25 46 99
1 Jno. ii. 27,	11 69
" iii. 14,	21
" iv. 18,	37
Rev. iv. 11,	37
" v. 8,	65
" viii. 3,	65

www.ingramcontent.com/pod-product-compliance
Lightning Source LLC
Chambersburg PA
CBHW022143160426
43197CB00009B/1414